THE LITTLE BOOK OF THE
1970s

Stuart Hylton

Illustrated by
Martin Latham

In memory of Pat Herington
1946–2014

First published 2015

The History Press
The Mill, Brimscombe Port
Stroud, Gloucestershire, GL5 2QG
www.thehistorypress.co.uk

British Library Cataloguing in Publication Data.
A catalogue record for this book is available from the British Library.

ISBN 978 0 7509 5975 9

Typesetting and origination by The History Press
Printed in Great Britain

Contents

Introduction and Acknowledgements

This is my fourth contribution to the *Little Book of* ... series, and each time I find myself using this space to explain what the book is not. It is not a learned and authoritative history of the decade. Many excellent books already perform that function, as I am about to acknowledge. It is intended rather to be something you can dip into and out of, as the mood and the topic take you. It combines (in its own way) some of the subjects a serious history of the period might cover, with others that it definitely would not. Where, for example, in the *Oxford History of England* do they discuss the influence of glam rock or Play-Doh?

When were the 1970s? It is not as silly a question as it might appear, for the series of events that might define the decade do not fall conveniently into years starting 197-something. Francis Wheen's excellent book about the paranoia of the decade, *Strange Days Indeed*, offers us several possible starting points. One definition might be when the passive utopianism of the 1960s gave way to a harder-edged reality, in which case 9 August 1969 (when actress Sharon Tate and friends were brutally murdered by Charles Manson and his disciples) or 4 May 1970 (when peaceful anti-war demonstrators at Kent State University, Ohio, were shot dead by what were presumably pro-war state troopers) might be candidates. Sports fans might settle for 9 March 1971, when Mohammed Ali was defeated by Joe Frazier (each man looking remarkably like the torch-bearer of the different sporting ideals of their respective decades). Believers in progress through technology might look to 3 April 1973 as the start of modern times, when the first hand-held mobile-phone call was made, whilst others will look back to 22 June 1971, and the opening of the Oz trial, as the start of an attempt by the establishment to claw back some of the changes wrought in the liberal (or depraved, depending on your view) 1960s.

Suffice it to say that we will not be confined by dates. If something looks as if it had an impact on the decade, whether it happened before, during or since the years concerned, it qualifies. Space, rather than chronology, is the real constraint in a book of this nature. Any serious student of the period wanting a fuller picture of the decade will also be amply rewarded by Dominic Sandbrook's admirable volumes *State of Emergency* and *Seasons in the Sun*, or Andy Beckett's *When the Lights Went Out*, to name just three of many worthy candidates.

My fundamental aim has been to provide some reminders of the decade in all its rich variety for those of us who were there and, for younger readers, to give you some clues as to why your parents turned out to be the weird old codgers that they undoubtedly are.

Stuart Hylton, 2015

1

As Seen on TV

Mass television ownership had been established by the 1970s. Nine out of ten of the population described viewing as a major leisure activity. But with only three channels to choose from, no video recordings and with computer games in their infancy, people were much more likely to be watching the same programmes. Thus they became part of the cement that bound the nation together, with shows like the Morecambe and Wise Christmas specials attracting audiences of well over 20 million.

The seventies were the decade of colour television. It first became available in 1967 but by 1970 only 1.7 per cent of the population had one. Colour started outselling black and white in 1974 and by the end of the decade there were over 11 million colour sets out there; only three out of ten households were still watching in monochrome. Many of those early sets were rented, since they were very expensive to buy (up to £400, or several thousands in today's money).

To begin at the beginning, what were the tiny – and not so tiny – tots watching in the 1970s?

When We Were Very Young

Captain Pugwash first appeared in black and white in the 1950s, but the colour television series ran between 1974 and 1975. It told of the adventures of Captain Horatio Pugwash and the crew of the

Flying Pig. They were incompetent pirates who were constantly getting into scrapes, often involving their arch-rival, Cut-Throat Jake of the *Flying Dustbin*. More often than not Tom the Cabin Boy, the one member of the crew who had his wits about him, would get them out of trouble.

One of the series' lasting claims to fame is the urban myth that the programme had characters with sexually explicit names – Roger the Cabin Boy, Seaman Staines and Master Bates. This story is thought to have originated in 1970s rag magazines, but when in 1991 the *Guardian* and the *Sunday Correspondent* reproduced it as if it were fact, John Ryan, the creator of the programme, successfully sued them.

What actually was crude about it was the animation of the series, which was done by cardboard cut-outs of the characters or other bits of the scenery being slipped in and out of shot in real time. Speech was animated by moving a piece of cardboard in front of the characters' open mouths. The animation was almost as primitive on *Ivor the Engine*, except that they used stop-frame techniques to move the cardboard cut-outs. The series was produced by Oliver Postgate, and was filmed in a cowshed at his home. It tells the story of Ivor, a small green steam engine who operates on a rural railway in the 'top left-hand corner of Wales'. His driver, nominally, is 'Jones the Steam' – except that Ivor, being a very wilful little engine, can travel under his own steam without human assistance, can speak, and is strongly inclined to break railway regulations. His lack of respect for the rules gets him into trouble with Dai Station, the station master, who is a stickler for them.

Ivor even sings in the Grumbly and District Choral Society, having had his whistle replaced by three organ pipes for the purpose. If you think it odd for a railway engine to be in a choir, one of the choir's other members for a time was Idris, the red Welsh dragon. The nation's heritage railways naturally cottoned onto Ivor. A small industrial locomotive was given a makeover to look more like Ivor and went on to make personal appearances around the country.

Stop-frame animation also featured in the series *Bagpuss*, produced in 1974 by Peter Firmin and Oliver Postgate. Only thirteen episodes were ever made, but in 1999 it won a BBC poll for the favourite children's programme and in 2001 even managed to come fourth in a poll organised by the rival Channel 4. It is set in a shop (more particularly in a shop window) in late Victorian times. The shop is run by a little girl called Emily, who does not actually sell anything, but displays broken and lost objects for their owners to collect and repair. The first part of the story is told in sepia photographs, as Emily shows her latest found object to Bagpuss, a knitted stuffed cat who lives in the shop window. When Emily departs, Bagpuss and the other characters in the shop window come to life, and sepia photographs give way to stop-frame animation. The characters discuss the new object, then repair it for the owner to collect.

Very few programmes for small children have a character based on the philosopher Bertrand Russell, but *Bagpuss* had Professor Yaffle, played by a woodpecker bookend (an imaginative if obscure piece of casting). This clearly impressed the University of Kent, for in 1999 they awarded honorary degrees to Firmin and Postgate. The two nominees said the award was really for Bagpuss, who was subsequently to be seen in academic dress.

If *Bagpuss* has a Bertrand Russell character, at least *The Wombles* have a large library of books left behind by human visitors to their home, Wimbledon Common. They also have a leader, Uncle Bulgaria, who is an avid reader of *The Times* (and thus, by definition, almost an intellectual). The Wombles have their origin in a series of children's novels, written by Elizabeth Beresford and published from 1968. They concern a race of pointed-nose furry creatures who live underground (they are everywhere, but the stories centre on those beneath Wimbledon Common).

The books turned into a children's television series, first shown between 1973 and 1975, a series of novelty records, a feature-length film in 1977 and even a rude football chant based on a

Wombles record ('Underground, overground, wandering free, the w*****s of Manchester City are we'). But unlike many football fans, the Wombles are useful members of society. They spend their time collecting and recycling the rubbish humans leave behind. Understandably, they have a pretty low opinion of humanity (with some exceptions, such as the Royal Family – you never see Her Majesty throwing away her McDonald's wrappings). That is why they keep well hidden from us. The name 'wombles' comes from a mispronunciation of 'Wimbledon' by one of the author's children.

Speaking of mispronunciations, what is the link between the children's programme *The Magic Roundabout* and one of the most famous French presidents? The television programme was originally French and there was a conspiracy theory in that country that it was in some way a satire of French politics. When it was remade in Britain, the central character was renamed Dougal and those same conspiracy theorists assumed that it was a none-too-subtle anglicising of the name de Gaulle.

The French series proved difficult to dub into English (particularly since the perfidious French neglected to supply the scripts along with the visuals). The BBC therefore redubbed it, using scripts written and performed by Eric Thompson (Emma's father) which bore precious little resemblance to the originals. It went out in 441 five-minute episodes between 1965 and 1977 (in colour from 1970), drew audiences of up to 8 million and attracted a fanatically devoted following. One theory is that at least part of the adult (or more precisely, student) audience watched it while stoned and saw psychedelic implications in it that the rest of us missed.

It was a puppet show, set in a magic garden, and used stop-frame animation and a cast of colourful characters. In addition to Dougal (a grumpy terrier), they included Zebedee (a jack-in-the-box), Brian (a well-meaning but simple snail), Ermintrude (a matronly cow), Dylan (a hippy rabbit) and Florence (a young girl). The show generally used to close with Zebedee saying 'Time for bed', which, given that the show went out before the six o'clock news, was far too early a bedtime for any viewers other than the stoned students.

Tiswas and Swap Shop

Tiswas started life on ITV in 1974 as a series of links between filler programmes such as cartoons, but soon proved more popular than the programmes it was linking and became a Saturday morning children's programme in its own right. Hosted between 1974 and 1981 by Chris Tarrant, it also became a vehicle for Lenny Henry, Jim Davidson, John Gorman (formerly of *The Scaffold* group), Jasper Carrott and ventriloquist Bob Carolgees and his punk dog puppet Spit. It consisted of a mixture of film clips, pop promos and general insanity, with the audience being doused in water and anyone, including the cameramen, liable to catch a flan in the face. This latter was felt by management to set a bad example, and was nearly banned. Testament to its popularity with an adult (or, at least, fully grown) audience came from the successful tour the programme did of the university campuses.

The BBC recognised the popularity of its rival and in 1976 brought in Rosemary Gill of its *Blue Peter* team to revitalise its Saturday morning broadcasts. The result was *The Multi-coloured Swap Shop* (or just *Swap Shop* for short). Running from 1976 to 1982, it was presented by Noel Edmonds, with help from Keith Chegwin, Maggie Philbin and, adding a much-needed bit of gravitas, John Craven as its news and current (children's) affairs correspondent.

The central feature of the programme (which otherwise was a familiar round of music, celebrity appearances, competitions and cartoons) was the 'swaporama'. In this, a BBC outside broadcast unit would go to some sporting venue and children (on occasions, up to 2,000 of them) would turn up to swap their belongings. The venue would be one the BBC were going to cover for a sporting event that day in any case, making the cost of the OB team sustainable. Many other television favourites cut their teeth on the programme, including Philip Schofield, Sarah Greene, Mike Read and Andi Peters, not to mention the likes of Michael Crawford and Delia Smith, who was on hand to show the viewers how to make sausage rolls. Among its more bizarre participants were a stuffed toy dinosaur named 'Posh Paws' (almost *Swap Shop* spelt backwards) and someone called Eric, who lived among the studio rafters and used to lower the viewers' postcards down to the presenters in a plastic ball.

Swap Shop was apparently voted the most influential show ever by industry insiders in 1999. But its competition with its ITV rival even spread to the football terraces, with supporters chanting out the names of one or other of the shows against each other.

Magpie

The BBC's venerable flagship children's programme *Blue Peter* has been broadcast since medieval times (actually 1958). It was always very worthy, but rather dull and square – a bit like having your dad making a television programme for you as children (perhaps they could have called it *Blue Pater*?). But between 1968 and 1980 it had a commercial television rival – *Magpie*. This set out to be as worthy as the original (well, almost as worthy) but a bit more groovy. Instead of the likes of Peter Purves and John Noakes, its presenters included a former Radio 1 disc jockey, Pete Brady, and ex-Bond girl Jenny Hanley. It even had a genuine rock band (the Spencer Davis Group under an assumed name) to perform its signature tune. At its peak the show pulled in audience figures of 10 million.

One of the characteristics of a magpie is that it has a reputation as a thief, and one explanation of the show's name is that it completely stole the format of its competition. Certainly, the newcomer copied many of the features of the established BBC model. Its content included items on news, science and history, but it was leavened with more on pop music and fashion. It, too, had collections for good causes, but rather than collecting postage stamps and milk bottle tops, they relieved their viewers of their (or, more likely, their parents') hard-earned cash. *Blue Peter* had a steam engine named after it, so *Magpie* had to do the same (number 44806, now living under an assumed name on the Llangollen Railway). *Blue Peter* had pet dogs, and *Magpie* had as its mascot a pet magpie named Murgatroyd.

The competition between them could sometimes get heartfelt. *Blue Peter* was scripted, whereas the *Magpie* presenters were free to improvise. *Blue Peter* doyen Biddy Baxter said of their rival, 'they used to make the presenters arse around in a way that children found extremely embarrassing, and it was just a terrible mess'. One of the *Magpie* team responded that if their show was messy, then *Blue Peter* was just sterile. No reason was ever given for *Magpie*'s disappearance in 1980, though there are dark rumours of some unspecified 'boardroom politics' being involved.

When We Were Very Silly

So what were the grown-ups of the 1970s watching (at least, once *The Magic Roundabout* and *Tiswas* had finished?). The decade's viewers had mixed fortunes. Starting with comedy, on the one hand there was *Terry and June*, a domestic sitcom that took blandness to a new level. Terry Scott and June Whitfield played a middle-class, middle-aged suburban couple coping with everyday tribulations (in his case, often self-inflicted). It started life in 1974 as *Happily Ever After*. Following a change of writers in 1979, virtually nothing else changed but the name, and that for contractual reasons. The 'new' programme continued until 1987, despite its dismissal by the critics, and managed to achieve better viewing figures than the edgier alternative comedy shows, some of which lampooned it. The programme's apologists (they do exist) maintain that Scott is everyman and that male viewers in particular are seeing their lives played out in a comedic version, as wife, employer, life and even inanimate objects conspire against him.

Other equally gentle, but perhaps more highly regarded and durable comedies of the period include *Last of the Summer Wine*, following the antics of a group of Yorkshire pensioners and *Dad's Army*, following the antics of a group of Walmington-on-Sea Home Guard pensioners during the Second World War. But the decade also gave us one of the enduring classics of television comedy, *Fawlty Towers* (1975–79). These complex farces were faultlessly constructed and the characters superbly drawn and played; the dialogue crackles and there are memorable one-liners. Only twelve episodes were ever made.

The series is set in a Torquay hotel and based on a real-life character – apparently an unbelievably rude and snobbish man called Donald Sinclair (who John Cleese says was much worse than Basil Fawlty – apparently the staff used to lock him in his room to stop him annoying the guests). The Monty Python team stayed at his establishment and suffered at his hands, leading John Cleese (and his then wife and co-writer of the scripts, Connie Booth) to revisit the hotel and study him further. The result is Basil Fawlty, a hotel proprietor who is unbearable towards the guests, hopelessly henpecked by his wife (played by Prunella Scales) and frequently on the verge of a nervous breakdown. The character was given a trial run in a 1971 episode of *Doctor at Large* but the series itself nearly did not get made. The BBC executive who was shown the first script said of it, 'This is full of clichéd situations and stereotypical characters and I cannot see it as being anything other than a disaster.'

Even Bill Cotton, the Head of Light Entertainment, could see nothing funny in the script he was shown, and it was only the fact that he trusted Cleese that made it possible for the show to go ahead. Most inexplicably of all, even the critics did not get the joke at first, having seen the televised finished result. The *Evening Standard* called it 'thin and obvious', the *Listener* 'Pretty hollow' and the *Mirror* headlined its review 'Long John short on Jokes'. But, in a later poll of industry insiders organised by the British Film Institute, they voted it the greatest television programme of all time.

One way and another, we were nearly denied such classic lines as:

Basil, talking about waiter Manuel: 'You'll have to forgive
him, he's from Barcelona.'

Basil, advising the staff on dealing with German guests:
'Don't mention the war.'

Basil: 'We used to laugh quite a lot.'
Sybil: 'Yes, but not at the same time, Basil.'

Basil: 'Don't be alarmed. It's only my wife laughing.'
(Elsewhere he likens the sound of her laughter to someone
machine-gunning a seal.)

Basil: 'Next contestant Mrs Sybil Fawlty from Torquay.
Specialist subject: the bleeding obvious.'

One show, which had started controversially in the 1960s,
continued on British screens until 1975 (its American offshoot
was launched in 1971 and for a time topped their ratings between
1971 and 1976). *Till Death Us Do Part* mocked the racism and
bigotry of the comedic monster Alf Garnett. Mary Whitehouse
predictably missed the point and complained about the profanity
of the leading character, and some even saw him as the not-very-
silent voice of Britain's silent majority, despite him invariably
getting the worst of any argument.

The 1970s also gave the television audience one of the most
original playwrights of that, or any other, decade. In *Pennies from
Heaven* (1978), Dennis Potter combines real-life drama with
explicit sexual activity and dark fantasies, in which the characters
burst into 1930s songs, all of it coloured by an exceedingly bleak
view of humanity. It is the story of Arthur Parker, a travelling sheet-
music salesman, and his unhappy marriage to his repressed wife

Joan (the role of Arthur made a star of Bob Hoskins). In it, he meets an innocent young schoolteacher, Eileen, who becomes pregnant by him and the plot steadily thickens and darkens thereafter. It later became a feature film and was voted twenty-first in a list of all-time greatest British television programmes in a poll in 2000.

Potter suffered from psoriatic arthropathy – a dreadful disease affecting his skin and joints – all his adult life, and it certainly coloured his view of the world. The skin complaint was a central theme of a later work, *The Singing Detective*, and the malaise generally influenced *Brimstone and Treacle*. This was produced in 1976, but not shown on television until 1987 (though it became a feature film and a stage play in the meantime). Alistair Milne, the Director General of the BBC who was instrumental in withdrawing it from broadcasting, described it as 'brilliantly made but nauseating'. The story involves a couple who care for a physically and mentally handicapped daughter, Pattie. A mysterious young man insinuates his way into their home and ends up raping the daughter. Potter acknowledged the impact of his illness on the work: 'I had written *Brimstone and Treacle* in difficult personal circumstances. [Years of illness] had not only taken their toll in physical damage but had also, and perhaps inevitably, mediated my view of the world and the people in it.'

If all this suffering were not enough, Potter would die of cancer in 1994, his final days made bearable only by a diet of brandy, liquid heroin and morphine.

But for those who liked their drama less demanding, there was always *Dallas*. This saga of a dysfunctional oil-rich Texas family, the Ewings, started life as a five-part mini-series. It ended up running for 357 one-hour episodes over fourteen seasons, between 1978 and 1991. In addition, the show spawned its own long-running offshoot, *Knot's Landing*, which also ran for fourteen seasons. No doubt for reasons of dramatic tension, the entire extended family lived together under the same roof (South Fork Ranch) when logic told you that, with their money, they could have afforded separate homes, particularly given that everyone seemed to hate everyone else in the household. The story starts when younger brother Bobby marries Pam Barnes, a member of the family that are the Ewings' sworn enemies. But gradually the action focuses on his corrupt and scheming elder brother, J.R., the real master at upsetting people.

The series were famous for their cliff-hangers and, when J.R. got shot at the end of the third series, there were about fifteen people in the frame with a motive for having done it. It kept viewers and betting syndicates gripped for months. (In case you were still wondering, it was J.R.'s sister-in-law, Kristin). The show is also notable for one of television's most feeble denouements to a storyline, when the entire ninth series was written off as having been a dream on the part of Pam Ewing.

One of the show's more unusual claims to fame is that it (allegedly) helped to bring down the communist regime in Romania. President Ceausescu allowed it to be shown there, thinking that all the feuding and back-stabbing would send out an anti-capitalist message. He could not have been more wrong. Viewers aspired to the affluence and freedoms portrayed in it (in marked contrast to their own circumstances) and it helped fuel the revolution. The pilot episode of *Dallas* was apparently one of the first programmes rerun on free Romanian television after Ceausescu's execution.

It was a decade when the image of the police on television was changing. On the one hand, *Dixon of Dock Green*, that throwback to the 1950s and before, continued until 1976, with Jack Warner (who was eighty by the time the last series came out) and his colleagues dispensing kindly justice in an idealised and relatively gentle East London community. On the other, you had harder-edged shows like *Softly Softly* (1966–76) giving a good deal more realistic take on policing in the modern world, and a far more realistic view of policemen as ordinary human beings. It was set in the fictitious Bristol suburb of Wyvern.

Harder-edged still was *The Sweeney* (1975–78), portraying the Flying Squad (Sweeney Todd = Flying Squad. Get it?) as a hard-drinking, womanising bunch of law-benders (if not breakers) who liked nothing better than a car chase leading to a punch-up and forty-eight pints. Interestingly, it was shown at a time when the real-life Flying Squad was itself in a lot of trouble for bribery, corruption and links with the criminal underworld. Their head, Detective Chief Superintendent Kenneth Drury, went down for seven years for said offences in 1977.

Lest it appear that the British police had it all their own way, America gave us *Starsky and Hutch*, a pair of California-based detectives with their hip informant Huggy Bear. But the real star of the series was of course their car, a red Ford Torino with highly distinctive white stripes along each side (ideal for under-cover surveillance). The two stars would jump over its bonnet rather than walk around it, or drive it madly round the fictitious suburb of Bay City, where the series was set, crashing through the piles of empty cardboard boxes with which every corner of the street was evidently littered.

The cars in real life were not noted for their performance, so Ford changed the back-axle gearing on theirs to give at least some low-speed acceleration. As a result, the car had a notice on the dashboard saying 'Do not exceed 50 m.p.h.' for fear of over-revving the engine and blowing it up. In the pilot show, the high-performance engine noises had to be dubbed on afterwards, to get around California state environmental legislation that prevented the cars being tuned. According to the Chief Constable of Merseyside, *Starsky and Hutch* had a tremendous influence on his staff. Apparently all his plain clothes officers started turning up for work in sunglasses and copycat versions of the duo's clothes. They also took to 'driving like bloody maniacs'.

The series predictably spawned a feature-length film version and action figure dolls. And if you doubt that the car was the star, collectors now pay $30–40 each for the human action figures, whereas their model car – if you can find one – might set you back $500.

'Jiggle TV' was a term coined in the 1970s by an American television executive, to describe television programmes in which young ladies jiggle their moving parts for the gratification of the (overwhelmingly male) audience. A jiggle TV programme consists of the following essential elements: (1) leading roles played by glamorous and improbably pneumatic young women (some of whom were surgically enhanced for the purpose); (2) scanty costumes, which allow the jiggling to be appreciated to its greatest advantage; and (3) a plot which necessitates jiggling, and may be far-fetched but not so complicated as to distract the audience from (1) or (2). One of the best-known examples shown in Britain was *Charlie's Angels*, in which three glamorous detectives investigate crimes, and where their undercover work frequently requires the angels themselves to be distinctly under-covered. Other examples include *The Bionic Woman* and *Wonder Woman*.

Jiggling was also a sub-plot in *The Dukes of Hazzard*, a story of good ole southern boys where the main characters' cousin, Daisy Duke, frequently strutted her admirable stuff in order to obtain inside information or to throw pursuers off her cousins' trail. Critics of such shows claimed that it was exploitative of, and patronising to, women. But their supporters argued that the characters the women played were not only picturesque but also smart, and that for women to break through into the previously male-dominated world of leading roles was a step forward. As to whether the women were chosen purely for their looks, it could equally be argued that most leading men did not exactly rival the elephant man in the ugly stakes. But Charlie's Angel Farrah Fawcett was in no doubt as to the reason for her success: 'When the show was number 3, I figured it was our acting. When it got to be number 1, I decided it could only be because none of us wears a bra.'

One British sub-group of the genre were the 1970s dance groups Pan's People, Legs and Co. and Hot Gossip. In the days before pop videos were commonplace, programmes like *Top of the Pops* used dancers to interpret the hits of artists who were not available in person. They became known (and admired in certain quarters) for their risqué costumes and routines, and the fact that they were a dance troupe gave them the perfect pretext for jiggling. They knew they must be doing something right when television campaigner Mary Whitehouse called for them to be banned. One small cross they had to bear were the parodies, with (among others) Benny Hill giving the world the all-male drag act *Pam's People* and the Goodies responding with the pensioner group *Pan's Grannies*.

Commercially seductive as jiggling may appear, it is not an automatic guarantee of success. When ITV decided to put on one of the leading examples of the genre, *Baywatch*, the BBC scratched its collective head to work out what to run against the considerable charms of Miss Pamela Anderson. What they came up with was reruns of *Dad's Army*. Everyone thought it was no contest, until the viewing figures came in. The final score was: Californian summer beach 7 million, 1940s Walmington-on-Sea 10 million.

2

Sequins and Safety Pins: 1970s Music

For some reviewers of 1970s popular music, it is enough to divide it into three parts – punk, glam/prog rock and disco. Other more discerning analysts say this is a wholly inadequate basis for looking at the rich variety of genres that the decade threw up. However, what we have here is a little chapter in a little book of the 1970s. So all we have space for is a brief review of the biggest names of the decade (and even here, I have had to limit myself to some home-grown products, rather than the overseas imports), along with a slightly more detailed exploration of the decade's most unique musical form. Apologies if your particular favourites are omitted, but there were a lot to choose from.

Glam Rock, Disco and Pop:
Some Stars of the 1970s

The Bay City Rollers

This band started life in Edinburgh in 1967 doing Beatles covers. After several changes in personnel they made their breakthrough in 1971 as the darlings of a teenage and pre-teenage fan base, with hits like 'Bye Bye Baby' (the biggest-selling single of 1975), 'Shang-a-Lang', 'All of Me Loves All of You' and 'Give a Little Love'. 'Rollermania' was assiduously promoted, with 'the tartan teen sensations from Edinburgh' – with their fashion choice of half-mast tartan trousers and matching scarves – becoming one of the many groups to claim the title of 'the greatest band since the Beatles'. Their manager summarised their appeal: 'The kids want to be happy and go along to a concert where they can scream, wet their knickers and have a really great time … I mean, isn't that what music's all about?'

Eat your heart out, J.S. Bach. Reviewers likened their concerts to Nuremberg rallies, though the level of casualties would have been unacceptable to Hitler, with young girls being crushed, trampled underfoot and treated for hysteria and shock. As is so often the case, the band's moment of glory was brief: by 1977 their star was beginning to fade and they stopped touring in 1981.

With such a fan base, the band naturally cultivated a squeaky clean image. Equally naturally, the media poked around, trying to find some good mucky scandal that would tarnish that image. They did not have to look too hard. Leaving aside drug and alcohol problems, one band member was charged with reckless driving, after knocking down and killing an elderly widow; their manager Tam Paton was gaoled for indecent acts with teenagers and heavily fined for cannabis dealing; another group member starred in a porn movie; one died of an AIDS-related illness and two band members attempted suicide. But, despite it all, a new version of the band (with just one original member) was still touring in 2013.

Slade

This band, originally from Wolverhampton and Walsall, was the most successful British group of the 1970s, based on their singles sales. They had seventeen top twenty hits in the early 1970s, including six Number 1s (three of which entered the charts at Number 1). Just one of these – 'Merry Xmas Everybody' – has sold over 2,500,000 copies alone, and their album *Slade Alive!* spent fifty-two weeks in the British album charts. The band started life as the 'N Betweens, but changed their name as a condition of getting a record deal (apparently 'Slade' was the name of the brand of shoes worn by one of the secretaries at the record company. Had the weather been different, we might have been talking about the 'Flip-flops'). Their dress sense was as striking as their music – for Slade were at the cutting edge of what passed for fashion among the glam-rock fraternity. Vocalist Noddy Holder favoured mutton-chop whiskers and a mirrored top hat, while Dave Hill appeared to have had his entire wardrobe supplied by a clowns' outfitter and then chosen which combinations to wear in a darkened room. Equally striking were their deliberate misspellings of their song titles, such as 'Mama Weer All Crazee Now', to the fury of educationalists.

Their fortunes waned somewhat in the latter part of the 1970s and they had an unsuccessful attempt to break into the American market. At one point, Dave Hill was reduced to using his own Rolls-Royce as a wedding hire car, to pay the bills. But things picked up again after Slade were a smash hit at the 1980 Reading Festival, as last-minute stand-ins for Ozzy Osborne. The band claim a wide range of influences for their music, from jazz guitarist Django Reinhardt to blues harmonica player Sonny Boy Williamson, and the bands who claim in turn to have been influenced by them are an equally diverse bunch, including grunge bands such as Nirvana, glam rockers Kiss and Motley Crue, mainstream pop groups such as Oasis, right through to punk bands such as the Ramones, the Sex Pistols and The Clash.

In 2000 Noddy Holder was awarded an OBE for his 'services to music' (though, for anyone who has been bombarded by 'Merry Xmas Everybody' each festive season for the last forty years, it leads you to question the sanity of the honours system). A version of the band (with just two of its original members) continues to tour to this day.

Elton John

Better known to his mother as Reginald Dwight, Sir Elton Hercules John, CBE (Why Hercules? Apparently he adopted the name in commemoration of the carthorse in the television sitcom *Steptoe and Son*), has had a career stretching over fifty years and is one of the most successful popular musicians of all time. He has sold over 300 million records and had over fifty Top 40 hits, and his 'Candle in the Wind' is the biggest-selling single of all time, with 33 million sales worldwide.

We include him in a book about the 1970s because the period 1970–76 is thought to have been his most successful, both artistically and commercially. He has six albums in *Rolling Stone*'s *500 Greatest Albums of all Time*, all of which date from this period. During the period 1972–75 alone he set a record by having seven consecutive albums reach Number 1 in the American charts. By this time, he was also becoming famous for the ever-more elaborate costumes that he wore to concerts and social events. Simple understated outfits involving sequins and ostrich feathers gave way to $5,000 pairs of spectacles that spelt his name out in lights and outfits variously portraying him as the Statue of Liberty, Mozart or Donald Duck. Not for nothing did he become known as the 'Liberace of rock and roll'.

He showed his talent as a musician at an early age, winning a junior scholarship to the Royal Academy of Music at the age of 11, but when he expressed a desire to follow music as a career his father tried to get him to take up something safe and well paid, like banking. Even as a successful banker, he would have struggled to make much more than he has from music – in 2011 he was said to be worth £195 million.

But even someone as successful as Elton John has known failure. He was auditioned for, and rejected by, both King Crimson and the Spencer Davis Group. More devastating still was his appearance before the BBC's Talent Selection Group, gatekeepers of

access to the corporation. He played them three songs and their conclusions were: 'The items are not songs. Pretentious material, self-written and sung in an extremely dull fashion without any feeling and precious little musical ability. Thin piercing voice with NO emotion. Not a tuneful voice ... He writes dreary songs and he sounds like a wonky singer.'

In the interests of balance, it should be reported that their conclusions were later overruled by their bosses, and that this cloth-eared Talent Selection Group also rejected David Bowie, the Rolling Stones, Marc Bolan and The Who.

In addition to his music, John is keen on football, supporting Watford. In 1976, rather than buy a season ticket, he bought the club. Bankrolled by him, and under Graham Taylor's management, the club went from the old third division to the first (younger readers, think First Division to Premier League). He sold the club in 1987 but remains its lifetime president.

He is also known for his charitable work. After some of his friends died of the disease, he set up a foundation to fund research into AIDS, which has so far raised over $200 million for the cause. His knighthood in 1998 was as much for his charity work as his music. He also played at the funeral of Princess Diana and appears to be a regular feature at any royal occasion when Her Majesty feels the need to 'get down wiv de kids'.

Led Zeppelin

Seen by many as being as influential in the 1970s as the Beatles were in the 1960s, Led Zeppelin's origins go back to when session guitarist Jimmy Page joined the Yardbirds in 1968. The group were already tiring of touring and, when they played their last gig in July of that year, Page and the band's bass player Keith Dreja were given permission to use the band's name to fulfil its outstanding obligations. They brought in Robert Plant, vocalist with a band called Hobstweedle, and John Bonham, drummer with Band of Joy; when Dreja also dropped out, session man John Paul Jones completed the new line-up on bass and keyboards. They played their first gigs as the New Yardbirds and the name Led Zeppelin was apparently suggested by The Who's drummer Keith Moon, it being his prediction of how the new band would be received. The New Yardbirds became Led Zeppelin in late 1968.

Their first album was released in January 1969, and already critics were calling them 'a significant turning point in the evolution of hard rock and heavy metal'. The single 'A Whole Lotta Love' was released the same year and sold over a million copies, and the band pursued a gruelling schedule of tours and recording. As their fame and wealth grew, so too did their reputation for excess and outlandish behaviour of all kinds. They hired their own airliner and took to booking entire floors in hotels which, from time to time, they would trash. Bonham was known to ride a motorcycle through them and, in July 1969, a Seattle hotel was the venue for the 'Shark Incident'. All I can tell you about it in a wholesome family publication such as this is that it involved a groupie and a large fish, and that the group say the incident has been exaggerated in the retelling, but they were barred from the hotel.

Their fourth album, released in 1971, was untitled and did not even bear the name of the group on the cover. This was said to be in response to unfavourable reviews of their work by some of the critics. But, despite this, it became one of the most successful albums of all time, selling over 37 million copies. Similarly, their tour venues grew ever larger. In 1973 they beat the Beatles' Shay Stadium record attendance, by playing to 56,800 fans in a stadium in Tampa, Florida. By 1975 they were the world's Number 1 rock and roll attraction and played to their largest crowd, estimated at 104,000, at the Knebworth Festival. Their musical influences expanded well beyond their original blues base, taking in the British, Celtic and American folk revivals (as Jimmy Page came under the influence of British acoustic guitarist Bert Jansch), world music, jazz, reggae and a host of others. (It seems that music pundits can take most ground-breaking acts and find influences ranging from Wagner to the 'Hokey Cokey' in their music). Led Zeppelin in turn became hugely influential on others – musically, in their mode of dress, in the way they operated in the music industry and even with their big hair. Over the course of their career they have sold anything between 200 and 300 million records and have been showered with every industry honour imaginable. In addition, Page got an OBE for his charitable work and Plant a CBE for his services to music.

Perhaps inevitably, the excesses of their lifestyle took their toll. In September 1980, after a long day spent taking liquid refreshment (his breakfast started with four quadruple vodkas) John Bonham was put to bed at Jimmy Page's Windsor home. He was found dead in the morning, having choked on his own vomit. The band decided he was irreplaceable and broke up. There have been occasional reunions since, at one of which Bonham's son Jason took his father's place behind the drums.

Queen

In 1970, guitarist Brian May and drummer Roger Taylor were playing together in a London band called Smile. When one of the band left, they brought in a friend, Farrokh Bulsara (later to become Freddie Mercury), as vocalist, and bass player John Deacon later completed the line-up. It was Freddie who suggested the change of name to Queen; he was at pains to point out its regal associations, though he was well aware of its other connotations.

Their first albums, imaginatively titled *Queen* (1973) and *Queen II* (1974), were generally well received, but not everyone loved them. *Melody Maker* reviewed *Queen II* as follows:

> The band with the worst name have capped that dubious achievement by bringing out the worst album for some time. Their material is weak and over-produced ... As a whole it is dire. Brian May is technically proficient, but Freddy Mercury's voice is dressed up with multi-tracking. A lot of people are pushing Queen as the band of '74. If this is our brightest hope for the future then we are committing rock and roll suicide.

But it was their third and fourth albums, *Sheer Heart Attack* (1974) and *A Night at the Opera* (1975) that really grabbed the public's attention and won them international fame. The latter was the most expensive album ever made at the time, largely because it featured the most expensive pop song ever recorded; 5 minutes 55 seconds-worth of 'Bohemian Rhapsody'.

It nearly did not get released as a single; record executives thought it was too long to get any airplay. The group only got around this by making bootleg copies available to Kenny Everett and other disc jockeys: the resulting public demand forced the company to release it. It truly was a massive enterprise – several years in gestation, three weeks to rehearse and three weeks to record, using five different studios. Some sections had as many as 180 over-dubs, stretching the technology of the day to its limits. For good measure, it was accompanied by a ground-breaking pop video, one of the first of its kind.

Was it worth it? The public certainly thought so. It had nine weeks at Number 1 in the charts (with a second spell after Mercury's death from an AIDS-related illness in 1991). It has won all sorts of accolades and was voted by the public as the greatest pop song of all time. After selling huge numbers as a single and as part of the *Night at the Opera* LP, the *Greatest Hits* LP on which it featured became the best-selling album in British pop history, outselling the Beatles' *Sgt Pepper's Lonely Hearts Club Band* by 604,000 copies. That just leaves one question: what on earth was 'Bohemian Rhapsody' all about?

There is a whole corner of the internet devoted to speculation on the subject. It was written by Freddie Mercury, and many of the theories revolve around him exorcising his personal demons. One has it that he was trying to come to terms with his sexuality (he was in a long-term relationship with a woman at the time, but had just embarked on a homosexual affair). Another says he was struggling with the loss of his mother and/or his religious faith (he had been brought up a Zoroastrian – an ancient Persian religion, based on the conflict between Ormuzd, the god of light and good, and Ahriman, spirit of darkness and evil, since you ask).

One theory that can be safely dismissed is that it had anything to do with AIDS, since the illness was barely known at the time the song was released, and Mercury was years away from being diagnosed with it. A completely different line of speculation is that it was an operatic realisation of Albert Camus' novel *The Outsider*. When the *Greatest Hits* album was released in Iran, the sleeve

notes (in Persian) gave an Islamic explanation of it, which said, 'the young man has actually killed someone and like Faust has sold his soul to the Devil. On the night before his execution, he calls for God in Arabic and, with the help of angels, regains his soul from Shaitan (the Islamic equivalent of Satan).' 'Bismillah' – a word familiar to devotees of the song – is the first word in the Qu'ran (Koran) and translates as 'in the name of Allah'. Or you may prefer Freddie's own explanation: he variously told people that even he did not know what the song meant, or that it was just 'random rhyming nonsense'.

Whatever the explanation, *Melody Maker* predictably did not like it. They said it 'contrived to approximate the demented fury of the Balham Amateur Operatic Society performing the *Pirates of Penzance*'. Their criticism had little impact on Queen's career, in the course of which they sold between 150 and 300 million albums (including eighteen Number 1 hits) and became one of the world's greatest stadium bands, playing in front of a record 150,000 audience at a free concert at Hyde Park in 1976.

The Bee Gees and Disco

What is *disco*? The term originates from the 1940s, when American radio popularised the term 'disc jockey' or 'DJ'. In occupied wartime France, restrictions imposed by the Germans meant that jazz clubs had to rely on recorded music, rather than live bands. These clubs came to be known as *discothèques*. Discos as we know them emerged in the United States in the 1960s, often frequented by African-Americans, Hispanics, gays and other minorities. They were said to be a reaction to the dominance of rock music in the mainstream media and what was seen as a rejection of dance music by those media. It is also suggested that these were venues where such minority groups could feel safe while 'doing their thing'.

Discos gave rise to their own musical genre, featuring lush arrangements and soaring vocals but, most of all, music that lent itself to dancing. Much of this music was American, but some British acts, notably the Bee Gees, featured among its hit groups. ABBA were the most important mainland European disco act. In addition, many other pieces of music, from pre-disco standards and the theme to the television show *I Love Lucy*, to Beethoven's fifth symphony and Rimsky-Korsakov's *Flight of the Bumblebee*, also got the disco treatment. The popularity of disco was greatly widened by the 1977 film *Saturday Night Fever*, whose soundtrack was one of the biggest sellers of all time.

Disco spawned its own wide range of fashions among its hard-core followers, encompassing bell-bottom trousers, platform shoes, jumpsuits, hot pants, halter dresses and double-knit leisure suits. Loud patterns, gold lamé and sequins were everywhere and bling jewellery was de rigueur. As someone put it, 'you could only fit in by wearing clothes that stood out'. Feminists denounced the revealing and sexual content of the ladies' fashions, but its supporters argued that it was actually a product of feminism, 'rejecting all the constructive garments of the past to show off the body as it is'. The men's wardrobe, whilst sometimes sexually ambiguous if measured against conventional standards, was equally positive, according to its champions like Yves St Laurent, who said, 'The spirit of the new generation of men is more liberated. They don't have the fear of not being virile.'

Disco also had its own pharmacopoeia – drugs primarily designed to enhance the sensation of dancing – cocaine, amyl nitrate ('poppers') and Quaalude, a drug originally developed for insomnia, but whose illegal, recreational use could also produce euphoria and increased sexual arousal (along with other potential side-effects, such as death).

The end of the 1970s saw a major decline in the popularity of disco in America. A Disco Demolition Night at Cominsky Park, Chicago in 1979 even turned violent, leading to extensive damage to the stadium and many arrests. Various reasons for this decline were speculated. One put it down to racist and homophobic motives among its opponents, given that gays and racial minorities were among the original champions of disco. Another conspiracy theory had it that the music industry were behind it, because they were finding it difficult to make enough money out of disco and it was harming their other popular-music markets. A third school of thought simply believed that the hedonistic lifestyle of disco fans had taken its toll of them. But disco survived and transformed itself into house, techno, hip-hop and a host of other terms incomprehensible to those above a certain age.

That's what disco is – so who were the Bee Gees? They were three brothers – Barry, Maurice and Robin Gibb, born on the Isle of Man but settled in Manchester until the late 1950s, when they emigrated to Australia. They began their musical career there but returned to Britain, with its bigger market, in January 1967. There they came under the influence of impresario Robert Stigwood. He hit upon the cunning idea of sending out their new single 'New York Mining Disaster 1941' with nothing on the record but the song title. Some disc jockeys mistakenly assumed it was a new release by the Beatles and gave it heavy airplay, helping to propel it into the Top 20. The group's career was under way and this was the first of a number of hits for them.

Their career was somewhat in the doldrums by the 1970s. They moved to Florida and were encouraged to turn their song-writing skills from ballads to more up-tempo disco numbers. Their fortunes were transformed by their involvement in the soundtrack of the film *Saturday Night Fever*. The film and its music were a huge worldwide hit, selling over 40 million copies and remaining at Number 1 in the American album charts for twenty-five weeks. It breathed new life into disco, which had itself become fairly moribund before then.

In the course of their careers, the Bee Gees sold some 220 million records, but their latter years were marked by tragedy. In 1988 their younger brother Andy, who was due to join the band, died from heart problems aged just 30. Maurice suffered a fatal heart attack in January 2003, at the age of 53, and Robin died of liver cancer in May 2012. Just about everyone in the music industry seems to have covered one or more of their songs and the list of their admirers includes such luminaries as Paul McCartney, Michael Jackson and Brian May of Queen.

But now we turn to the musical form for which the decade will be most remembered (fondly or otherwise).

Punk

Various explanations can be found for the emergence of the 1970s phenomenon that became known as punk. Sociologists might attribute it to the alienation of young people from a society that seemed to be falling apart, and which offered them very poor prospects, and not much to do while they were waiting for those meagre prospects to materialise. Arty types might point to the influence of a host of stylistic influences, including nihilism, Dadaism, anarchism and the situationists (who believed that bourgeois society could be undermined by putting on outrageous and offensive public spectacles). But Al Spicer, the editor of the *Rough Guide to Punk*, has a more down-to-earth explanation for it: 'a meaty combination of teenage rock 'n' rollers, art students with a yearning to be noticed and fashion designers hoping to sell a heap of very expensive trousers'.

But let's start with the music. By the 1970s, some audiences were getting pretty fed up with rock and roll. A genre which had started out as edgy, with Elvis's gyrating pelvis deemed too stimulating to be shown on television, had become stodgy. Middle-of-the-road acts like Simon and Garfunkel and Billy Joel, however good they may be in their own right, were being misleadingly marketed as rock. Outstanding artists like Jimi Hendrix were being copied by pale imitations; interminable guitar (or worse, drum) solos and a thick layer of pretention could not disguise the poverty of some of the material.

Moreover, the very fact that some of these stars were richer than God alienated them from parts of their impoverished fan base. By 1982, ABBA had overtaken Volvo as Sweden's biggest earner of foreign currency, and, as one reviewer put it, the mainstream pop press was just as likely to focus on Fleetwood Mac's fleet of cars and boats, Queen's taste in antique furniture or Hall

and Oates' real estate investments as they were the bands' music. Life for many ordinary young people was very different. In the summer of 1977 some 104,000 school leavers went straight from school to the dole queue and, by the end of the decade, four out of ten under-25s were unemployed.

As a reaction, home-made bands started to make their own stripped-down music that went back to the roots of rock and roll. They drew inspiration from, among other things, some of the 1960s minimalist hits, like the Kinks' 1964 'You Really Got Me' and 'All Day and All of the Night', the Troggs' 1966 'Wild Thing' and The Who's 1964 'I Can't Explain'. These amateur bands called their music 'garage', at a time when many commercial so-called rock and roll bands were much more 'drawing room' than 'garage'.

Another suspect feature of the commercial product was just that – its commercialism; it was over-produced, over-packaged and over-marketed. Many would-be performers were suspicious of this glitz and looked to record, produce and distribute their music themselves. Another thing they dispensed with, in some cases, was the need for talent. As one editor of an early fanzine put it, the new music was 'rock and roll by people who didn't have very much [sic] skills as musicians but still felt the need to express themselves through music'.

Taking it back to its fundamentals, *Sideburns* fanzine published three diagrams of guitar chords with the instructions, 'this is a chord, this is another, this is a third. Now form a band.' Some of the music literally was that basic, a twelve-bar, three-chord format with solo playing cut down to a minimum, the guitars driven at a relentless pace to generate a hypnotic buzzing noise and the vocals often shouted rather than sung. Anyone who tried to sophisticate this recipe ran the risk of being labelled a poseur. This was by no means the first flowering of home-made music: the popularity of skiffle in the 1950s and the various rebirths of folk music across the decades are all testaments to people's desire to be music-makers, rather than just consumers.

One of the early leaders of this new kind of basic music was the New York band, the Ramones. Someone who heard them there was the British entrepreneur Malcolm McLaren, while he was in the city, trying (and failing) to manage another band, the New York Dolls, with a view to using them to promote a range of clothing. His decision to get the cross-dressing, foul-mouthed New York Dolls to pose in red patent leather outfits in front of a Soviet flag flew in the face of just about everything middle America held most dear.

On his return to London, McLaren planned to set up another band to promote the range of fetishistic fashions, sold through the King's Road boutique called SEX that he ran with his clothes designer partner, Vivienne Westwood. He formed the Sex Pistols from a group of youths who used to congregate there, some of whom already played in a band variously called The Strand or The Swankers. As vocalist, they recruited someone who has been described as a 'wild-eyed green-haired yob' with 'sadly sporadic dental hygiene' called John Lydon. His stage name 'Johnny Rotten' referred partly to his abilities as a singer and partly to the state of his teeth.

They performed their first gig at the Saint Martin's School of Art on 6 November 1975. From the start, the band said they were more into chaos than music, and they went out of their way to provoke a violent reaction from the audience, abusing them ('Bet you don't hate us as much as we hate you!' shouted Johnny Rotten at his audiences), spitting ('gobbing') on them and diving from the stage into the audience, with the risk of injury to audience, band member or both. Future band member Sid Vicious was arrested at one concert for throwing a glass at the audience and putting a girl's eye out with it (he would later top that by allegedly murdering his girlfriend and then topping himself with a drug overdose before the case came to court). In February 1976 the band went a stage further in their riotous behaviour, trashing London's Marquee Club, including the sound equipment of Eddie and the Hot Rods, who were supposed to be following them on stage. Thereafter, they were rarely asked to play the same venue twice.

The opportunity to offend a wider audience presented itself on 1 December 1976, when teatime television presenter Bill Grundy ill-advisedly provoked the band into exposing the viewers to the full extent of their vocabulary. Their expletives ensured that many of the band's subsequent tour bookings and record promotion engagements got cancelled, and EMI dumped the band in January 1977, as a lack of live shows and broadcasting bans led to disappointing record sales. The interview also effectively wrecked Grundy's television career, though it is now regarded as a classic by those who like that sort of thing, and is frequently repeated for their benefit. The broadcast brought the Sex Pistols national notoriety and the outrage turned their live performances into something more akin to freak shows than musical events. In their own way, they were every bit as theatrical as the glam rock and prog rock that they professed to despise.

At this time, merely displaying the Sex Pistols' wares had its risks: a Nottingham shop that put their record *Never Mind the Bollocks, Here's the Sex Pistols* in its window found itself prosecuted under the 1889 Indecent Advertisement Act. Needless to say, in the 1977 *New Musical Express* readers' poll, the Sex Pistols won every category in which they could conceivably be entered (Johnny Rotten as 'Most Wonderful Human Being'?! Some mistake, surely?).

They called the new style of music 'punk'. The term had been around since Shakespearian times, and had indeed been used by the great man in his play *Measure for Measure* to mean a prostitute. In early twentieth-century prison slang, it was used to describe a passive male homosexual, and it evolved into 'a young male hustler, a gangster, a hoodlum or a ruffian' – in other words, a term representing just about the lowest form of life any film or television detective could encounter (ask Dirty Harry), which suited the punks just fine.

New bands swiftly followed the lead of the Sex Pistols. The Clash and The Damned formed from the break-up of another band, London SS, before it had even performed in public. The Clash hung about with a group of followers of the Sex Pistols called The Bromley Contingent, described by Julie Burchill as 'a posse of unrepentant poseurs, committed to attaining fame'. From them emerged The Slits, Siouxsie and the Banshees, Generation X and X-ray Specs. A Sex Pistols concert in Manchester in June 1976 was attended by fewer than a hundred people, but it brought together the people who would go on to form Joy Division, The Fall and (later) The Smiths.

Predictably, punk was not universally popular. Charles Shaar Parker of *New Musical Express* reviewed one concert and concluded, 'The Clash are the sort of garage band that should be speedily returned to the garage, preferably with the motor still running',

while the Ramones picked up publicity in Scotland, not for their music, but for a glue-sniffing death linked to them (one of the tracks on their LP was called 'Now I Wanna Sniff some Glue'). With a few exceptions, punk made little impact on the charts – only thirty-eight punk singles even made the Top 30 during its 1977–78 heyday, and the genre never built a huge audience outside its main fan bases, such as the art colleges. The top-selling disco recordings outsold the most popular punk by a ratio of about forty to one.

The lyrics of punk, whether barked or shouted, are worthy of mention. They looked to get away from the pastoral idylls of the hippies and the sentimental, not to say pretentious, verbiage of some of the prog rock music of the day. They dealt bluntly with the problems of urban life, unemployment and relationships, in a way which challenged the values of the establishment and authority. The Sex Pistols even brought out their own 'national anthem' 'God Save the Queen' (this in the Silver Jubilee year of 1977). It got to Number 1 in the charts, despite (or possibly because of) being banned for its offensiveness by the BBC, but also coincided with members of the band being attacked in the street, by outraged (and in one case knife-wielding) monarchists. Generally speaking, however, any political content of punk was relatively unfocused – it was more an attitude than a message, a scream of frustration and hopelessness, but one that did not offer any solution.

The movement also had a range of fashions, behaviours and values attached to it. Selling the look, you will remember, was Malcolm McLaren's original *raison d'être*, more than the music. The approved form of attire started out as jeans and leather bomber jackets, and graduated into ripped clothing held together with safety pins, clothes pegs and bondage straps. (Bondage trousers, for those who like that sort of thing, have the lower legs fastened together by straps.) Haircuts could be short crops that appeared to have been done with a rotary lawnmower or, at the more manicured end, the spectacular Mohawk, in all its multi-coloured variety and with unemployability guaranteed (they can still be seen on tourist postcards, and now form part of Britain's heritage). They also had their own dance – the pogo, or jumping up and down as we would call it. Not exactly graceful, but easy to learn. Too easy, perhaps, because the masses pogoing at an Ian Dury and the Blockheads gig at the Ilford Odeon caused the dance floor to give way.

With many artistic forms that set out to outrage middle England, the establishment has a way of drawing them to its ample bosom and squeezing all the shock out of them. So it was that the symbolic end of punk as an instrument of horror came in June 1979, when Johnny Rotten appeared with Joan Collins on BBC's relentlessly middle-of-the-road *Juke Box Jury*, voting on whether this or that bubble gum pop single would be a hit or a miss. Worse still, the commercial fat cats had belatedly cottoned on to the fact that there was money to be made from punk, and were busy buying up and marketing its leading exponents – and if there was anything guaranteed to turn off the protesting youth who had first breathed life into the movement, it was that. Its obscurity had been the very thing that guaranteed its authenticity.

Epilogue: The Home Secretary Rocks

The 1970s saw the golden age of the free music festival movement, when hordes of people would assemble to listen to rock music, smoke jazz cigarettes and make sweet music with members of the opposite (or possibly the same – after all, it had been legal since 1967) sex. The idea of a free festival started by accident at the Isle of Wight in 1970, when the fences separating ticket holders from the rest got uprooted and it was suddenly open to all. An intentionally free festival was held that same summer at Worthing, a town normally associated more with Vera Lynn than with heavy metal, and the first free festival at Glastonbury in 1971 attracted some 10,000 people.

The queen was the unwitting (and no doubt unwilling) host to a free festival in Windsor Great Park in 1972, organised by a former civil servant turned LSD consumer named William Dwyer. The police arrived in the area but only about 700 people turned up, and the event went off peacefully and dispersed quickly. It was a different story the following year, when Dwyer staged a repeat performance. This time the audience numbered between 10,000 and 20,000 and both they and the police were more hostile towards each other. Almost 300 arrests for drug offences were made and the police only refrained from closing it down after nine days because of a lack of officers. In 1974 the police tried fencing off the park to keep vehicles out, but still the crowds came. Dwyer's publicity leaflets openly encouraged defiance of the police and the drug laws: 'If two people, smoking dope, are approached by the police, they may well piss in their pants from fright … In a crowd of 1,000 all smoking dope together, you can tell the police to piss off.'

By the sixth day, the event was getting high-profile media coverage. The police decided that this 'gigantic drug-inspired breach of the peace' had to end. Early in the morning they entered the site en masse and started turfing the festival-goers out. The official line for the festival-goers, called for from the stage, was non-provocation and non-violence. Some of the festival-goers interpreted this as meaning to throw bottles and cans at the police, who responded with a generous application of the truncheon. The police concluded their eviction by rocking the flimsy stage until it collapsed.

Dwyer was still determined to stage a 1975 festival (and was later gaoled for trying to do so). Meanwhile the government was hatching up the wacky idea of cooperating with elements in the free festival movement to stage an official free festival somewhere less sensitive. They formed an improbable alliance with Sid Rawle, a professional counter-culturalist who had been a member of just about every anti-establishment group going and who had earned himself the title of 'king of the hippies'. He too had been imprisoned at the time for illegal festival promotion, but at least he spoke a language the officials could understand – he described a free festival as 'a trade fair for alternative lifestyles'.

They found a site – Watchfield, a disused wartime airfield in Oxfordshire, not far from Swindon. It was owned by the Department of the Environment and, best of all, the local MP was Airey Neave, the close confidant of Margaret Thatcher. Who better for a Labour government to annoy? He was gratifyingly outraged and said he would get the ombudsman to investigate this use of taxpayers' money. Local villagers sent a petition of protest to the Home Secretary (regardless of the fact that the festival had been his idea in the first place) even as the arrangements went ahead.

By 23 August, all the elements of a town for 20,000 people were in place. It had a nursery, a chapel, its own radio station and newspaper, car parks, covered sleeping space in a disused hangar, a theatre, a cinema and accommodation for 450 policemen and

their helicopter, while the alternative society laid on a long list of bands from among the usual suspects who frequented such events. On day one, the weather was bad and only 5,000 people had turned up but, over the nine days of the festival, both the weather and the crowds picked up. Fake LSD was on sale, but for anyone with the real thing a hut was set aside for those having a bad trip, where they could fuel each other's paranoia. The event was mostly good natured and as lawful as these events ever can be; the police kept a low profile and some Hell's Angels provided such law enforcement as they thought necessary.

The local residents, who had originally threatened a mass exodus, were sufficiently intrigued to look in, and may have been treated to the spectacle of women sunbathing topless on the grass. Readers of tabloid newspapers certainly saw them. Even Airey Neave visited and seemed reconciled. He described it as 'very orderly' and said he would like to see a permanent site provided, so long as it was 'self-financing and not an imposition on local villagers' (that is to say, somewhere else). But his wish was not to come true. Despite a largely favourable government post-mortem on the event, it was announced early in 1976 that the government would not be financing any further free festivals. Severe budget constraints were cited as the reason by the government – or was it because Airey Neave had seemed to enjoy it too much? Further unofficial people's free festivals were held around the country in 1976, 1977 and 1978 but, facing ever more efficient local opposition and dwindling audiences, interest in them petered out.

3

A Decade of Disasters

Sadly, no decade is without its disasters. Here are some of those with which 1970s Britain was afflicted.

Moorgate Tube Crash

At 8.46 a.m. on 28 February 1975 a southbound Northern Line underground train passed through Moorgate station at 30–40 miles an hour. The problem with this was that Moorgate was the terminus on the line, which ended in buffers and a brick wall some 20 metres beyond the station. The six cars making up the train concertinaed and, of the 300 or so people aboard, forty-three (including the driver) were killed and another seventy-four had to be treated in hospital.

The cause of the accident remains a mystery to this day. No mechanical fault was found in the train. Such was the carnage inside the tunnel that it took four and a half days to get the driver's body out. During that time, decomposition of his body had started to set in, making it difficult to establish whether he had been incapacitated in some way. No evidence of a stroke, heart attack or anything similar could be found. He did have a blood alcohol level of 80mg per 100ml (which would be illegal for a motorist) but this may have been the result of chemical changes in the body after his death. He was said to have been a very light drinker.

Suicide was also considered, but it turned out that he had plans to buy a car after he finished his shift, and was carrying the money for it when he died, suggesting that suicide was unlikely.

The accident led to the introduction of safety measures to slow any train entering a terminus at excessive speed.

Ibrox Stadium Disaster

It was an old firm match, Rangers at home to Celtic on 2 January 1971. It had been a dull game right up until the ninetieth minute, when Celtic scored what seemed to be the last-minute winning goal. Hordes of disappointed Rangers supporters started making for the exits. But as they were making their way out, a roar went up inside the ground. Against all expectations, Rangers had scored an equaliser in extra time.

There are differing accounts as to what happened next. One version has it that somebody – possibly a father carrying a child – slipped on the stairs, starting a chain reaction. Another says that some of the departing fans tried to turn round and go back in, to see what the cheering was all about, and came up against the crowds pushing to get out. Whatever the cause, hundreds of fans were sent tumbling down the stairs, landing with such force that the safety railings were twisted completely out of shape. Bodies were piled six deep in some places, the life crushed out of them by the sheer weight of numbers. Sixty-six people were killed and over 200 injured in what was to be Britain's worst football ground accident until Sheffield's Hillsborough disaster of 1989. Among the dead were five schoolmates from Fife, four of them from the same street.

This particular stairway – stairway 13 – had a track record. In September 1961 two people had been killed and seventy injured in a similar crush, and there had been non-fatal incidents in 1967 (eleven injured) and 1969 (twenty-nine injured). Despite £150,000 having been spent on ground improvements, an inquiry held Rangers to be responsible, and sixty families of the deceased sued the club. The accident led to the Safety of Sports Grounds Act 1974, requiring local authorities to inspect sports stadiums and issue safety certificates. But it would take the Hillsborough disaster, and the Taylor Report that flowed from it, to provide a comprehensive review of safety.

Eltham Train Crash

Sunday, 11 June 1972 was to have been a jolly day out at the seaside for the employees of the London Midland Railway and their families. A special excursion train had been laid on from Kentish Town to Margate. Once he had dropped his passengers off, the driver stabled his train at Ramsgate and had the afternoon free until he made the return journey. He went off to the pub for beer and thereafter to somewhere else, where he drank sherry. That afternoon, the driver clocked back in by telephone and headed back to collect his passengers. His guard noted a hint of alcohol on his breath, but that did not stop the pair of them going for three pre-journey pints at the railway social club.

The driver was still not displaying any signs of intoxication when they set off, for he was known among his friends as a man who could hold his drink. However, once they got going, the guard noticed his speed was somewhat excessive and his braking 'intense'. The guard tried to alert him to this but, before he could, they reached Eltham. There is a sharp bend in the tracks at Eltham. The reason for this is that the Victorian landowner of the Well Hall Estate wanted the line to skirt his property, so that the station could be built right on the edge of it. The maximum speed for this bend was supposed to be 20mph, but the driver tried to take it at about 65mph. The locomotive and nine of the ten carriages were derailed, some of them ending up on their sides. The driver and five passengers were killed and 126 people injured.

The cause of the accident was, for once, easy to find. The driver's blood alcohol level was about three and a half times the legal limit for

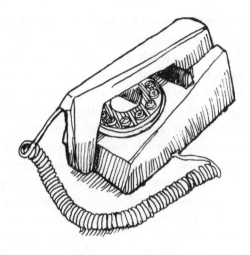

a car driver. The pathologist estimated that he had drunk about five and a half pints of beer, one-third of a bottle of sherry and quarter of a bottle of spirits, and it was thought that he had even been drinking whilst in the cab. Changes were made to the signalling at Eltham, to give drivers additional warning to slow down, and there was criticism of the arrangement for clocking on by telephone, which meant that the driver's drunken state had not been spotted sooner.

Bloody Sunday

This term was originally used to describe events in Tsarist St Petersburg in 1905, when Russian troops opened fire on a crowd of unarmed, peaceful demonstrators who were marching to the palace to present a petition to the tsar. In its modern, Irish context it refers to what is sometimes called the Bogside Massacre of 30 January 1972, where twenty-six civil rights protesters and casual onlookers in Derry were shot by members of the British Army. Thirteen were killed immediately and another one died later of his injuries. Seven of those killed were teenagers and, of the wounded, five were shot in the back. None of them was found to be armed.

The background to this was that there was discrimination on a range of issues (electoral boundaries, voting rights and the allocation of public housing) against Northern Irish Catholics in the 1960s. This led a body called the Northern Ireland Civil Rights Association (NICRA) to mount a campaign against it. They were non-violent, but were secretly sponsored by the IRA, no doubt in the hope that civil unrest would grow from it and aid in the removal of the Unionist government. But a campaign of violence escalated in parallel with the peaceful protest and, in August 1971, the government gave itself powers to intern people without trial. At the same time, parades and demonstrations were banned. (This latter measure was aimed particularly at the provocative Protestant Apprentice Boys' marches).

NICRA decided to challenge the ban on demonstrations and organised a march through Derry. It was felt that a march to the Guildhall area could be too provocative and the organisers instead agreed to march to Free Derry Corner, which was unambiguously Catholic territory. But a small breakaway group tried to reach the Guildhall. They threw stones at the police and army guarding the route and were met in turn with water cannons, tear gas and rubber bullets. The authorities had brought in military reinforcements to help police the event. The 1st Battalion, Parachute Regiment had a reputation as some of the hard men of the British Army and it was they who started firing live rounds into the crowd. The victims included people waving white flags of truce, people trying to get away from the trouble, those trying to help the wounded and some who were not even part of the demonstration.

An inquiry was commissioned into events on that day. It was chaired by Lord Chief Justice Widgery and reported just eleven weeks after the events of 30 January. It took the side of the army in almost every particular, accepting their story that they had been responding to demonstrators who had been shooting at them and throwing nail bombs, though the evidence to support this is notable for its absence. The strongest criticism he would make of the army was that their behaviour 'bordered on the reckless'.

His report was accepted at the time by the government and by some Protestant groups in Northern Ireland, though it outraged the Catholic community and was to prove an impediment to a peace settlement for decades to come. It is now generally accepted to have been a shameless whitewash and is discredited.

Such was the dissatisfaction with Widgery that Lord Saville was asked to conduct a further inquiry into the events in 1998. Nobody can accuse Saville of hurrying out his conclusions, for his report did not appear until 2010. It acknowledged that the troops' actions had been 'unjustified and unjustifiable' and potentially opened the way to further legal action against individual troops. It further concluded that the troops had fabricated evidence to back up their version of events. The prime minister accepted this new account of events and made a public apology on behalf of the United Kingdom when the Saville Report was published. Bloody Sunday and its aftermath poisoned relations between the British government and the Northern Irish Catholic community for decades.

Markham Colliery Accident

Markham Colliery, at Staveley, some five miles north-east of Chesterfield, was a major local employer. Its 1,870 underground and 425 surface workers produced 30,000 tons of coal a week and 30 July 1973 began like any other working day. The colliers were loaded, up to thirty-two at a time, into their cage for the 1,400ft drop to their coalface. The cage was supposed to fall at about 20ft a second (13.6 miles an hour), controlled by a winding engine man and backed up by various safety devices. At about 5.35 a.m. the engine man saw sparks coming from the machinery and heard a bang. He immediately applied the brakes but neither they, nor any back-up measures, had any effect. It was estimated that the cage was going at about twice its recommended speed when it hit the bottom of the shaft. Eighteen of its occupants were killed and another eleven seriously injured.

Some of the injured had to be carried to another shaft 700 yards away to get them out, and it was two hours before the last of the casualties reached even the colliery's medical centre, let alone hospital. Horrific as it was, the disaster could have been a lot worse. Two cages were connected to opposite ends of the same winding rope and, as the 'down' cage plummeted to the bottom of the shaft, the 'up' cage smashed through the engine house on the surface. Miraculously, the 'up' cage was empty. An inquiry showed that a steel braking rod had sheared due to metal fatigue. Tests found that these rods were subject to far greater stresses than had been appreciated.

Markham Colliery was no stranger to disaster. In 1938 it had suffered an underground explosion that left seventy-nine dead and a further forty injured. It was finally closed in 1994.

Summerland Fire

The Summerland leisure centre on the Isle of Man opened in May 1971 and its promoters spoke highly of it. They called it a 'new concept in leisure' that would 'set the architectural world alight'. With hindsight, their choice of words could have been better. But even the British Tourist Authority called it an 'outstanding tourist enterprise'. The idea was to provide a holiday destination that the weather could not spoil. The 50,000-square-foot building on the Douglas seafront was kept at a constant 80°F and offered a dance floor, crazy golf, a waterfall and five storeys of leisure facilities, pubs and restaurants. One particular feature was the bronze-tinted clear acrylic sheeting with which the front and top of the building was glazed, and which was supposed to turn ordinary daylight into the appearance of tropical sunshine.

Up until August 1973 it was very successful, and on the evening of 2 August some 3,000 visitors and 200 staff were in the building. But behind all the glitter was a disaster waiting to unfold. Three of those present were boys from Liverpool, looking for somewhere to have an illicit smoke. They broke into a disused kiosk and, while smoking there, managed to set the kiosk alight. The boys fled, and it soon became clear that the building was a fire-safety nightmare. Two different firms of architects had designed the building and, if they had ever considered fire safety, they certainly had not liaised with each other to ensure that their parts of the building worked as a fire-protected whole. The burning kiosk fell onto the exterior wall of the building, which proved to have little in the way of fire retardant properties. The sound-insulation material inside the wall was even worse, and exploded, spreading the fire to the flammable cladding of the front wall and roof. The open-plan design of the building contributed to the holocaust, offering chimneys and unprotected air vents through which the fire could spread. As the acrylic roof burned, pieces of it rained down on the people below, starting more fires. There were, of course, no sprinklers.

As if the design of the building were not bad enough, its management also contributed to the disaster. Fire doors were padlocked, to stop non-paying visitors getting in. The staff had little or no training in fire drills and nothing was done to organise an evacuation until the scale of the blaze became evident, crowd panic took over and people started being trampled. Most extraordinary of all, they failed to call the fire brigade for thirty minutes. The alarm was only raised when the captain of a ship 2 miles out at sea radioed the coastguard and said, 'It looks as if the whole of the Isle of Man is on fire.' Soon, every fire appliance on the island was heading for the seafront at Douglas.

Fifty people died that night and another seventy-nine were injured. It was the second-worst loss of life through fire in the British Isles since the Second World War. Amazingly, what was left of the centre reopened for business eleven days later, and ghoulish holiday-makers actually queued to get in. But the damage to Summerland's reputation was terminal, and the remaining part of the centre was demolished in 1975. A smaller-scale replacement opened in 1978, but closed in 2004 and was demolished the year after.

Equally extraordinary was the fact that the inquiry into the disaster did not find any individual or organisation to blame for this catastrophe, though it did manage to criticise the delay in evacuating the building and the use of flammable building materials. Unsurprisingly, changes were later made to the building regulations governing such buildings. A disaster fund raised £85,000, from which the grand sum of £100 was paid to the next of kin of each person who died in the disaster.

More Trouble on the Tracks

The 17.18 express service to Oxford left London Paddington on 19 December 1973. It had just had its batteries recharged, but someone forgot to secure the door to the battery box. The door hit the platform at Ealing Broadway station, causing it to become even more detached, and allowing it to hit a point switching device. The points changed under the train, causing it to derail and go zig-zagging for hundreds of metres across all four tracks. Ten people were killed and ninety-four injured.

On 22 October 1979 the passenger service between Glasgow and Dundee was forced to stop alongside Invergowrie Bay when one of its motors caught fire. About ten minutes later the Glasgow–Aberdeen express ran into the rear of it at about 60mph. Four carriages of the Dundee service were thrown over the sea wall by the impact, two of them actually landing in the Firth of Tay (fortunately the tide was out).

Two possible reasons were advanced for the accident: one was simple driver error, with the driver of the express failing to see the stop signal. The other was a fault in the old-style semaphore signal, which could mean it giving an ambiguous message. However, we are unlikely ever to know, since both the driver of the express train and the colleague who was with him in the cab died in the accident (along with three passengers) and fifty-one others were injured.

On 6 June 1975, the sleeper service from London Euston to Glasgow passed through Nuneaton, where changes to the track were being made and a 20mph speed limit was in effect. Unfortunately the light illuminating the advance sign warning of the restriction had gone out, leading the driver to believe the restriction had been lifted. By the time he discovered otherwise, he was doing 70mph in the 20mph area and his train was falling off the rails. Six people were killed and thirty-eight injured, but the driver was found not guilty of manslaughter. The accident was instrumental in the introduction of the automatic warning system, which gives an audible advance warning of restrictions.

On 16 April 1979, the 19.50 train from Glasgow to Wemyss Bay went headlong into the service between Ayr and Glasgow, after the latter disregarded a red signal. It was thought the driver of the Ayr train was the victim of a 'ding ding and away' accident, where the guard or platform staff use a green flag or bell signal to send the train out, despite there being a 'red' on the trackside signal.

HMS Fittleton

HMS *Fittleton* was a wooden-hulled minesweeper, at one time known as HMS *Curzon*. She was launched in 1956 but, by 1976, was part of the Royal Navy Reserve. In September of that year, she was part of a Royal Navy force taking part in NATO manoeuvres in the North Sea. At one point she was required to come close alongside HMS *Mermaid*, but a bow wave caused them to come rather closer together than they had intended. They collided and, within a minute, the *Fittleton* had turned over and sunk. Survivors in the water were picked up and, the following day, a salvage vessel reclaimed the *Fittleton* and took it back to Holland for repairs. Five bodies were found on board, but a further seven were recorded as 'missing, presumed dead'. The *Fittleton* returned to service, but was scrapped the following year.

4

Naughty Boys

In this chapter we look at the careers of some of the naughty boys of the decade. All naughtiness is, of course, relative, and our list combines some relatively minor misdemeanours with more serious offenders, and some who are rather off the scale of naughty.

Mister Generous

John Poulson (1910–1993) was an architect who never got his professional qualification, claiming he was too busy to do so. After a period as a trainee, he decided to set up his own architectural practice. His former employer was not impressed with his design skills, telling colleagues, 'Have you heard that Poulson's starting on his own? Christ, he couldn't design a brick s***house!'

But he soon displayed his real ability, of cultivating contacts who might bring him work. He joined the Freemasons and developed links with the right-leaning National Liberal Party. He built his practice into an all-in-one service, covering costing, planning and construction. By the 1960s his company was one of the largest of its kind in Europe.

Newcastle was one of the cities looking to regenerate itself as wartime austerity eased, and the council's leader, T. Dan Smith, was in 1962 appointed as a consultant to Poulsons, essentially using his many contacts across the public sector in the north-east to secure

Poulson introductions. Poulson had realised that councillors could have huge financial clout in the council chamber but very modest means of their own – an ideal scenario for bribery. Poulson soon had a string of such 'consultants' across the region. He also made gifts to many up-and-coming civil servants, whose favours he then called in to secure him work for the nationalised industries. One civil servant with political expertise even moonlighted as Poulson's speechwriter.

Poulson's involvement with the National Liberals brought him into contact with senior government ministers, and Members of Parliament were the next group to be added to his payroll. Among the most senior of these was Reginald Maudling, the then Shadow Commonwealth Secretary, who became chairman of one of Poulson's companies. (For good measure, Maudling's son was also given a job by Poulson and one of his wife's charities received large donations from him.) Poulson was at the peak of his powers and, on the face of it, the very embodiment of respectability. He was a commissioner of taxes and his wife chaired the Yorkshire Women Conservatives.

Poulson's company was by now turning over about £1 million a year, but even so the cost of bribing a small army of councillors, local authority officers and civil servants was proving ruinously expensive. His tax situation was seriously out of control and in November 1968 the Inland Revenue obtained a judgement against him for £211,639. He was heading for ruin and filed for bankruptcy in November 1971. The hearings the following spring brought Poulson's financial affairs to the attention of the police, and they began a fraud investigation. Reginald Maudling was by then Home Secretary and the titular national head of the police. Despite the fact that he had resigned his position with Poulson, Maudling had used his influence to help secure Poulson work in Malta. His position was untenable and he was forced to resign.

In June 1973 Poulson was arrested for corruption. He denied all the charges, saying, 'I have been a fool, surrounded by a pack of leeches.' The judge saw it differently, calling him 'an incalculably evil man' as he sentenced him to five (later increased to seven) years in prison. Poulson's meticulous and detailed record-keeping proved particularly helpful to the prosecution. Many of his contacts, including T. Dan Smith, went down with him (Smith got six years). Only the Members of Parliament involved got off unscathed, courtesy of a legal loophole not available to the general public. The case has been called the largest public corruption scandal of the twentieth century, involving as it did twenty-three local authorities and 300 individuals, and it did much to colour voter opinion against free-spending local authorities in the north of England.

Poulson was released in 1977, one of the conditions of his release being that half the proceeds from his autobiography went to his creditors. Even then, the creditors would be frustrated, as the book was withdrawn and pulped by the publisher, for fear of libel actions by those named in it.

The Missing Member

John Stonehouse (1925–1988) was brought up in a socialist political environment – his mother was Labour mayor of Southampton – so it was hardly surprising that, after attending the London School of Economics, he decided to stand for Parliament. He contested Twickenham in 1950, aged just 25, and was elected MP for Wednesbury in 1957. He established his right-on credentials in 1959 by going on a fact-finding visit to Rhodesia and managing to annoy the white supremacist government of the day so much that he was thrown out of the country. Promotion followed, with him becoming Minister for Technology in 1967 and Postmaster General in 1968 (until the post was abolished when Labour lost the general election the following year). His constituency disappeared in 1974 but he got himself re-elected to nearby Walsall North.

As a sideline he had set up various companies, most of which were in financial difficulty by 1974. His attempts to solve the problem by creative accountancy caught the eye of the Department of Trade and Industry, and he resorted instead to creative identity, by adopting the alter ego of Joseph Markham, the dead husband of a constituent. To add to the complexity of the situation, his marriage was also in trouble, and his secretary, Sheila Buckley, was also his mistress. He took out a £125,000 insurance policy, payable to his wife in the event of his death, and on 20 November 1974 left a pile of clothes on a Miami beach. The assumption that he had drowned or been devoured by a shark was successful: he was presumed dead and obituaries were published, even as he was making his way to a new life in Australia. But his complicated arrangements for transferring large sums of money to Australia using false names caught the eye of an observant bank cashier – the police were informed and Stonehouse/Markham was placed under surveillance. Initially, the police thought he might be the fugitive peer Lord Lucan (of whom more shortly). One of the first things the police made him do, once arrested, was to drop his trousers, since Lord Lucan had a tell-tale 6-inch scar on his thigh.

His true identity was eventually discovered. Six months later he was deported to England, having tried and failed to get asylum in Sweden and Mauritius. On his return in June 1975, he continued to conduct his constituency MP duties from his prison cell in Brixton. Only on 7 April 1976 (three weeks before his trial) did he resign the Labour whip, with the result that Labour became a minority government. He was tried on twenty-one charges, including fraud, theft, forgery and wasting police time. He chose to defend himself and his success may be judged by the award of a seven-year sentence in Wormwood Scrubs.

His health deteriorated in prison, and he was given early release in August 1979 after three heart attacks and open heart surgery. His wife had divorced him, leaving him free to marry Sheila Buckley, and he also embraced the Social Democratic Party (later to become the Liberal Democrats). He worked as a charity fundraiser, wrote three novels and fathered a child, before his fourth, fatal heart attack on 14 April 1988.

Only after his death did it become public knowledge that he had been a spy in the pay of the Czech government since 1962. Accusations of this were first made in 1969, but he had successfully rebutted them. Margaret Thatcher and Cabinet members had known since 1979 that he had in fact provided the Czechs with information about government plans, as well as technical information about aircraft, for which he had been paid about £5,000. But since he was already in prison and there was not enough evidence to prosecute him with confidence, no public announcement was made until December 2010. We cannot end without clarifying Stonehouse's contribution to the cultural life of the nation – his disappearance was said by some to be the inspiration for the television comedy *The Fall and Rise of Reginald Perrin*, but the novel on which the series was actually based was written (though not published) shortly before Stonehouse's disappearance.

The End of the Peer?

Richard John Bingham (1934–?) was the 7th Earl of Lucan – Eton, Coldstream Guards, merchant banker, professional gambler, one-time candidate for the role of James Bond, Aston Martin driver, powerboat racer – and suspected murderer. He had married Veronica Duncan in 1963 but, nine years and three children into the relationship, the marriage collapsed. Lord Lucan lost a bitter custody dispute for the children and he moved out into a flat near the family home in Lower Belgrave Street. From there he conducted an obsessive stalking campaign against his wife, aimed at gathering evidence to win back custody.

At about 9.55 p.m. on 7 November 1974, a blood-soaked and distressed woman staggered into the Plumbers Arms, Lower Belgrave Street, crying that she had just escaped being murdered, but that someone had killed the family's nanny. It was Lady Lucan. Police entering the basement of their house found blood everywhere, including on a length of lead piping, and a sack containing the battered body of the nanny, Sandra Rivett. When she had recovered somewhat, Lady Lucan named her husband as the murderer. One school of thought has it that Lucan entered the house intent upon murdering his estranged wife as part of his campaign for custody of the children, but in the dark had mistakenly attacked the nanny.

Of Lord Lucan, there was no trace. Later that night, he telephoned his mother, saying there had been a catastrophe in the house and asking her to pick up the children but, by the time she got there, the house was already full of police.

About 11.30 p.m. that night, Lucan turned up at a friend's house in Sussex in a borrowed car, dishevelled and distressed. He told the friend that he had been walking past the family house when he saw through a basement window somebody assaulting Lady Lucan. He went in to try and rescue her, but slipped on some blood (which allowed the assailant to escape). He tried to comfort Lady Lucan, but she ran out of the house, crying 'Murder!' He had realised that things could look slightly incriminating for him, and had panicked and fled. His friend tried to persuade him to stay and go to the police with her, but he said he had to 'get back', and departed. It was the last validated sighting of him. Three days later, the borrowed car, complete with bloodstains and a length of lead pipe matching the murder weapon, was found at the ferry port of Newhaven.

The case naturally generated huge public and press interest and a massive manhunt. There were complaints of an 'Eton mafia' working against the police, and the mother of one of their number, Lady Osborne, told the police that Lucan had been fed to the tigers in her son's private zoo, prompting a futile search of the cages for clues. Fourteen other country houses and estates were also searched, again fruitlessly. The inquest concluded that the nanny died from head injuries that were inflicted by Lord Lucan. He was the first member of the House of Lords to be named a murderer since 1760, and the last person to be committed by a coroner to a crown court for unlawful killing; a coroner's power to do so was taken away by the Criminal Law Act 1977. Friends of Lucan still continued to argue his innocence, though there are many apparent flaws in the story he had told on the night of his disappearance.

Lucan's whereabouts remain a mystery to this day, though there is no shortage of theories. The simplest one seems to be that Lucan, guilty of the crime, did what he saw as the honourable thing and took his own life – possibly by jumping to his death from a boat in the English Channel. But plenty of people believe otherwise – and coincidentally these events took place within weeks of John Stonehouse's disappearance and rediscovery. Another claim was that Lucan was helped out of the country by shadowy financiers, who then judged him too great a risk, and had him murdered and buried, either in Switzerland or at sea.

A third theory has it that Lord Lucan is alive and in South America (or Africa, or possibly the USA, or could it be Canada?) One version of this theory is that he was flown out of the country to southern France from an airfield at Headcorn, Kent by his friends James Goldsmith and John Aspinall, before making his onward journey to his final destination (whatever that might have been). This school of thought also has it that he has even made several trips back to the UK since 1985. Naturally, Lord Lucan has been seen thousands of times, in just about every country in the world. As we saw, John Stonehouse was mistaken for him in Australia. A sighting in Columbia turned out to be an innocent American businessman; one in Goa, a folk singer from St Helens. Then there was the harmless British expatriate in New Zealand; and so on. But the theory about him having been seen riding the missing racehorse Shergar in the company of Elvis Presley may safely be discounted.

The Bunny Man

It is not every day that the leader of a major national political party, someone spoken of in certain circles as a potential future prime minister, gets involved in a seedy scandal involving unlawful sexual liaisons and attempted murder. Jeremy Thorpe (1929–)

was the charismatic and colourful leader of the Liberal Party at a time when it could well have held the balance of power in Parliament. From an early stage in his parliamentary career there were questions (or, in some minds, even certainties) about his sexuality, at a time when homosexuality was still illegal. In 1960 or 1961 he made the acquaintance of young stable boy with a history of mental illness, named Norman Josiffe. What started out as a normal piece of constituency business soon moved on to a sexual relationship, with Thorpe setting Josiffe up in a Chelsea bedsit, giving him money and helping him to find a job.

But Josiffe (or Norman Scott, as he went on to call himself) was greedy, ungrateful and paranoid. He formed the view that Thorpe had treated him shabbily and took his accusations about Thorpe's homosexuality to the police, which he substantiated with a series of letters that Thorpe had written to him. These accusations were drawn to the attention of the Home Secretary when Thorpe became leader of the Liberal Party in 1967, but no further action was taken. With the help of fellow Liberal MP Peter Bessell, Thorpe tried to silence Scott by paying him a weekly retainer.

Bessell was not the ideal co-conspirator, being a man with a series of dodgy business interests who had taken to embezzling Liberal Party funds to prop them up. Bessell alleged that in December 1968 Thorpe, fearful that Scott would bring his promising career crashing down, started talking about 'getting rid of him' and that it would be 'no worse than shooting a sick dog'. Thorpe always denied this, but Bessell further claimed that ever more bizarre plots were hatched to get rid of Scott, variously involving a hired assassin, poison, a Cornish mineshaft and the dumping of Scott's body in the Everglades, to be eaten by alligators.

Meanwhile, Scott was touting his story around anybody who would listen. The Liberal Party would not take him seriously, nor would the *Daily Mirror*. Eventually he got the ear of a freelance journalist named Gordon Winter, who also happened to be an informant for BOSS, the South African Bureau of State Security. Thorpe was an outspoken critic of the apartheid state and they decided to keep the information in reserve, planning to use it to destroy Thorpe in the event of an election where the Liberals held the balance of power.

Just such an event came to pass after the first 1974 election. Scott's persistent allegations and some investigative journalism led first to Thorpe resigning the party leadership, and then to him and three others being charged with conspiracy to murder Scott. The prosecution at the trial alleged that Thorpe decided to silence Scott permanently. The plot (if it existed) was comical in its amateurishness, with a young airline pilot named Andrew Newton being hired, either to shoot or simply to put the frighteners on Scott (depending on who was telling the story). The finance for it would come (strictly unofficially) from party funds. Newton lured Scott onto Exmoor, where predictably he made a hash of the job, shooting Scott's dog but the gun terminally jamming when he allegedly tried to see off Scott. Newton fled, leaving Scott weeping over his dog at the roadside.

The dead dog story got into the local newspaper, but was also picked up by *Private Eye*. Then Scott was hauled up before Barnstaple magistrates' court for benefits fraud, where he used the public forum to reveal his sexual relationship with Thorpe. Thorpe was forced into denying it and Prime Minister Harold Wilson (who by this stage was getting obsessed with conspiracy theories of his own) believed the story that it was all part of a plot by BOSS. He said so in the House of Commons.

But on 9 May 1974, the bundle of letters Scott had given the police years before somehow found their way into the *Sunday Times*. Among other things they revealed Thorpe's pet name for Scott – 'bunny' – not the sort of thing a chap called a chap, decided the court of public opinion. Thorpe resigned as Liberal leader the following day.

The net was closing in; Newton was arrested and got two years for possession of a firearm with intent to endanger life, and in October 1977 he sold his account of the assassination plot to the *Evening News*. The Director of Public Prosecutions studied this account with interest and, in August 1978, Thorpe and his alleged co-conspirators were summoned for conspiracy to murder. Thorpe consistently denied any wrongdoing, sexual or murderous. He continued to enjoy considerable support within his party and reneged on the promise he had made to his successor as Liberal leader, David Steel, to resign as an MP in the event of criminal charges being brought against him. The electors of North Devon finally settled this for him, voting him out at the 1979 election. That same election cost the Liberals dear, largely (it is thought) as a result of the Thorpe scandal. The Liberals lost almost 2 million votes to the Conservatives, helping to propel Margaret Thatcher into 10 Downing Street.

At the trial, the prosecution case depended largely upon the testimonies of the dodgy co-conspirators, all of whom managed to discredit themselves in the witness box in one way or another. It emerged that Bessell, for example, had sold his memoirs to a newspaper and that his fee would double if Thorpe were found guilty. Thorpe, by comparison, emerged as the very model of probity, aided by a judge who came across in his summing up as one of Thorpe's admirers. The defendants were found not guilty. Whether he was innocent or not, the political career of Jeremy Thorpe, who might have been Home Secretary in a coalition government in 1974, was over. Shortly after the trial he found that he had Parkinson's disease and retired from public life altogether.

The Art Man

Cambridge University has an almost unrivalled reputation for producing academics, thinkers, people who distinguish themselves in all sorts of ways – and Russian spies. Anthony Blunt (1907–1983) was one of their leading lights in the latter category, though his involvement only became public knowledge late in his life. He was the son of a vicar who was attached to the British Embassy in Paris, where as a child Blunt became immersed in the artistic culture of the city. After Marlborough College he won a scholarship in mathematics to Trinity College, Cambridge, where he joined a self-appointed elite group, the Cambridge Apostles. This secret society regarded themselves as the brightest minds in the university; many, including Blunt, were homosexual (then illegal) and Marxist (widespread among 1930s intellectuals, and legal but hardly more respectable than homosexuality in some circles). Academically, Blunt switched courses to modern languages, graduating with first-class honours in 1930. He went on to teach French at the university, and became a fellow of Trinity College in 1932, specialising in French art history.

Blunt visited the Soviet Union in 1933 and some say he was recruited the following year. Blunt would have it that Guy Burgess recruited him, but others suggest that Blunt himself was the talent spotter, identifying potential Russian spies for the NKVD. Blunt joined British intelligence when war broke out, serving in France and subsequently being evacuated in 1940. Shortly after, he was recruited to the security service, MI5. According to some, his involvement with the Russians may have been known about even then. Nonetheless, he was able to pass the Russians decrypted Enigma intercepts from the Russian front and details of German spy rings inside the Soviet Union. This created a huge risk of the Germans finding out about Britain's ability to decipher Enigma traffic, with the most serious consequences for the war effort.

By the end of the war, Blunt had attained the rank of major; he was sent to retrieve sensitive correspondence between the Duke of Windsor and Hitler, and was asked to help the Royal Librarian obtain some letters to the Empress Victoria (Queen Victoria's daughter and mother to Kaiser Wilhelm). He was by now distinguished as an art historian and, in 1945, was appointed Surveyor of the King's Pictures (a post which he held for twenty-seven years, under George VI and Elizabeth II). He became professor of the history of art at the University of London and a director of the Courtauld Institute of Art; he was knighted in 1956. His contribution to the world of art, at least, was considerable and survives unsullied.

Blunt's possible involvement with Russia was discussed in private in the immediate post-war years, but, with the defection of Burgess and Maclean, Blunt (a close friend of Burgess since Cambridge) came under closer scrutiny. He was interviewed a dozen times between 1951 and 1952 without revealing anything. MI5 finally got conclusive proof of Blunt's guilt (from the Americans) in 1963, and Blunt confessed the following year. In return for what he said was a full confession (including shopping a number of his fellow spies) he was granted immunity from prosecution and a fifteen-year promise of official secrecy about his activities.

Blunt's social standing appeared to be unaffected by this turn of events, until Andrew Boyle's 1979 book *Climate of Treason* was published, in which Blunt was represented as 'Maurice'. Blunt's attempt to stop the book's publication caught the attention of *Private Eye* and, through them, the public. Prime Minister Margaret Thatcher made two statements in the Commons about Blunt's wartime activities and he (and people associated with him) were hounded by the press. The queen stripped him of his knighthood and he was removed as an honorary fellow of Trinity College. Deeply shocked by his exposure, Blunt retreated from society. He died of a heart attack, aged 75.

His memoirs were passed to the British Library and made publicly available in 2009. In them, he claims that the Russians tried to get him to defect with Burgess and Maclean (which he refused to do), and says that spying for Russia was the biggest mistake of his life.

Serial Killers

In these last sections, we look at some of the most notorious serial killers of the decade, all of whom got whole-life sentences that meant they would never be released (that is, until the European Court of Human Rights ruled in July 2013 that whole-life tariffs were illegal. At the time of writing, the English courts' response to this ruling has yet to be fully tested).

The (Old) Lady Killer

Patrick Mackay (1952–) was the son of a violent alcoholic father, who died when Patrick was 10. At school he took to bullying the other children, arson and torturing animals (one of his first arson attacks was on the family's pet tortoise). By the age of 15 he was already being detained in a secure mental hospital for the attempted murder of his mother and an aunt; a psychiatrist described him as a 'cold psychopathic killer'. Like Moors murderer Ian Brady he was fascinated by Nazism and he followed his father in taking to the bottle. The authorities ill-advisedly released him (against the recommendation of the staff who had had direct dealings with him) in 1972. In February 1974 he forced his way into the home of 84-year-old widow Isabella Griffiths. Having strangled her, he had a good look around the house, then went back and stabbed her for good measure. The body was not found for twelve days.

He served a four-month prison sentence for theft from July 1974, in the course of which he planned a campaign of terror against little old ladies. After his release, he committed a series of attacks on them, fortunately without killing any of them. But in March 1975 he got into a hostel for elderly women and murdered Adele Price (89) by strangling her. Eleven days later, he went to Gravesend, where he came upon a priest, Father Crean, who befriended him. They had a falling out and, having already stabbed him several times, Mackay for some reason got really cross with him, and set about him with an axe. The priest's skull was shattered and Mackay watched him, horribly injured, bleed to death. The trail was easy for the police to follow and he was arrested within two days.

Although he was only ever found guilty of these three murders, Mackay owned up to eleven and the police think there may have been more.

The Black Panther

Donald Neilson (1936–2011) was another one who had a troubled childhood. He was bullied at school on account of his short stature and his name (his real name was Donald Nappey), and his mother died when he was 11 years old. He married at the age of 18 and his wife persuaded him to leave the army. Instead, he took up a career as a housebreaker, and is thought to have committed some 400 burglaries without being arrested.

In 1971 he decided there were better returns to be made robbing sub-post offices, and he is thought to have carried out some fourteen robberies between 1971 and 1974. In the course of these, in 1974, he carried out his first three murders, shooting two sub-postmasters and the husband of a sub-postmistress, as well as brutally beating up sub-postmistress Margaret Grayland. His nickname came about because of the speed at which he worked and the dark clothing he wore to carry out his crimes. In the mid-1970s he became Britain's most wanted man, after shooting a security guard six times – with the same gun that forensics found had been used to carry out the previous murders.

When a newspaper article appeared about a 17-year-old heiress called Lesley Whittle, Neilson saw another opportunity. He kidnapped her and demanded a £50,000 ransom. Due to various problems, the family were unable to pay the ransom in time. Lesley's body was eventually found at the bottom of a drainage shaft.

He was finally caught when he tried to hijack a police panda car at gunpoint. The officers eventually managed to overpower and disarm him. They were helped in this by the patrons of a fish-and-chip shop near where the car had stopped. In fact, the crowd took to disarming him so forcefully that Neilson had to be given police protection. He was given five life sentences, with a further sixty-one years thrown in for all his other crimes. Unsurprisingly, this amounted to a whole-life tariff and he died in custody in 2011 of motor neurone disease.

The Beast of Manchester

Trevor Hardy (1947–2012) was not a man to fall out with. Before the series of events that draw him to our attention, he served time for chastising a man with a pickaxe handle, in a row over a round of drinks. His reign of terror over north Manchester began at the end of 1974, overlapping with the first killings of the Yorkshire Ripper (of whom more shortly).

It was on New Year's Eve 1974 that he mistook a 15-year-old girl for someone with whom he was infatuated. He displayed his affection for her by stabbing her and burying her body in a shallow grave in the Manchester district of Newton Heath. Seven months later, his next victim was a 17 year old, walking home from work at night. She was hit with a brick, robbed, strangled and sexually assaulted. Hardy kept her bloodstained clothes and handbag as trophies but, when the police interviewed him, he had an alibi ready. He had even filed his teeth down to points, so they could not match bite marks on the woman's body.

This left him free to commit a further murder, of another 17 year old, whose body was found by the Rochdale Canal. By now, Hardy was on the run, living rough in a park, during which time he committed another serious (but fortunately non-fatal) sexual assault on a woman. He chose to conduct his own defence at his trial, pleading manslaughter on the basis of diminished responsibility. The judge was having none of it, and handed down three life sentences. Hardy then argued for these to carry a minimum sentence of thirty years, but the judge said it should be a whole-life tariff. And so it proved to be, with Hardy suffering a heart attack, from which he died, in Wakefield Prison in 2012. Shortly after his imprisonment, Hardy had written a letter to one of the victim's families, explaining that it was not his fault but that of his parents, for the way he had been brought up.

The Yorkshire Ripper
Peter Sutcliffe (1946–) was the product of a working-class Yorkshire Roman Catholic family. He left school at 15 and worked in a series of unskilled jobs, before training as an HGV driver. He married in 1974 and the couple bought a house in Bradford.

He had regularly visited prostitutes and in 1969 had assaulted one, hitting her over the head with a stone wrapped in a sock. Police tracked him down and Sutcliffe admitted the assault, but played down the level of violence involved. He got away with it, because the woman was not prepared to take the matter further.

He carried out a series of three attacks on women in 1975, being disturbed on each occasion and leaving them scarred, traumatised and seriously, but not fatally, injured. In October of that year, he committed his first murder, hitting a Leeds prostitute with a hammer and stabbing her fifteen times. A massive police hunt, involving 150 officers and 11,000 interviews, failed to find the culprit. His next victim was another Leeds sex worker, the following January, whom he hit with a hammer, stamped on and stabbed fifty-one times with a sharpened screwdriver. The press linked the two murders and coined the name the 'Yorkshire Ripper' for the perpetrator. The victim of his next attack, that May, survived and was eventually able to testify against Sutcliffe.

A series of attacks followed between February 1977 and November 1980, leaving a total of thirteen women dead and several others injured. Most, but not all, were sex workers in Leeds, Bradford, Huddersfield and Manchester. It is thought that Sutcliffe's hatred of them originates from an early dispute with one over money. But the fact that some victims were not sex workers led to fears that all women were potential victims. By now, some 300 police officers were working on the case, checking out thousands of cars and conducting 12,500 interviews. Sutcliffe himself was interviewed in 1978 – the first of nine questionings which failed to link him to the crimes. Meanwhile the police received – and were seriously side-tracked by – a recording and letters purporting to come from the murderer. The man had a Wearside accent and taunted the police, 'I'm Jack. I see you're having no luck catching me. I have the greatest respect for you, George [the officer leading the case], but Lord, you're no nearer catching me now than four years ago when I started.'

The search for this Wearside man diverted an enormous amount of police time, and it was not until 2005 that it was found to be the work of an unemployed Sunderland alcoholic, John Humble, who got eight years in prison.

Meanwhile, in 1981, Sutcliffe was stopped by the police in his car, in the company of a sex worker. His car was found to have false number plates and he was taken into custody. Further discoveries started to link him more closely to the Ripper crimes and, after two days of intensive questioning, he owned up to being the Ripper. Only one of the crimes did he not admit to, and this was later found to have been the work of a copycat. He described the attacks and told the police that God had told him to carry them out. Sutcliffe tried at his trial to plead manslaughter on the grounds of diminished responsibility, but the jury found him guilty of thirteen counts of murder. He was sentenced to life with a minimum term of thirty years, later extended to a whole-life tariff, under which he would never leave prison alive. Sutcliffe appealed this last verdict, but lost the case.

The police were strongly criticised for their conduct of the case. It was one of their largest-ever investigations and pre-dated the use of computers. Every scrap of evidence was written on cards and was very difficult to cross-reference. Also, undue attention was felt to have been given to the Wearside 'Jack' communications. The Inspector of Constabulary, Sir Lawrence Byford, produced a report on the conduct of the case in 1981. It was not published by the Home Office until 2006, and then only partially. It concluded that Sutcliffe was very likely to have been responsible for crimes other than those for which he was charged. A number were identified that fitted his modus operandi, but the police have never been able to charge him with them.

Having been found sane at his trial, Sutcliffe was later diagnosed as schizophrenic, and transferred from Parkhurst Prison to Broadmoor Hospital. Prisoners at both institutions have attempted to injure or murder him.

The case was naturally a gift to conspiracy theorists. One such has it that Sutcliffe was no more than a copycat; that most of the murders were carried out by a 'stocky bearded Irishman', whom the theorist names; that the 'Wearside' man was the real Ripper, and had put on the Wearside accent to throw the police off the trail; that the police gratefully accepted Sutcliffe's conviction, guilty or not, to clear up the case and carried out an elaborate cover-up of their many blunders. For good measure, this theorist also maintains that the real Ripper is still on the loose, and is looking to kill him.

The 'Kindly Killer'

Dennis Nilsen (1945–) was not brought to justice until 1983, but much of his gruesome murderous career took place in our decade. He was born in Scotland, of mixed Scottish and Norwegian parentage. Theirs was an unhappy marriage, which resulted in Nilsen spending part of his childhood with his grandparents. He would later claim that it was the trauma as a 6 year old of seeing the dead body of his much-loved grandfather that sent him over the edge.

In 1961 he joined the Army Catering Corps, in which he served until 1972. The skills he learned there would later come in useful, but not in any way the armed forces would wish to show in their recruitment advertising. By 1978 he was living in Cricklewood and his serial killing began. His targets were boys and young men, many of them homeless, homosexual or male prostitutes. He would befriend them in pubs or bars and take them home, where he plied them with food and alcohol, later murdering them by strangulation and drowning. He regarded this as a 'humane' form of execution, one which led him to bestow upon himself the title of the 'kindly killer'.

He would store the bodies for extended periods under the floorboards or in a wardrobe, sometimes fetching them out for necrophiliac sexual activity, or to sit and 'watch' television with him. He claimed that he was lonely, and could not bear the thought of his victims leaving. This way, their 'stay' could be extended. Eventually, he would be forced to dispose of them and he would use his army butchery skills to chop them up, before burning them on a piece of waste ground behind the flat. He would add pieces of rubber to the bonfire to disguise the smell of burning flesh. Entrails were thrown over the garden fence for the wildlife to eat.

In 1981 he moved to a flat in Muswell Hill. This had neither floorboards, beneath which to hide his victims, nor waste ground on which to burn the evidence. Neighbours began to notice the funny smell in the flats, as Nilsen stored his victims in bin bags. Eventually he took to boiling them up, to remove the flesh, which he could then flush down the toilet. In time this blocked the house's drains, and it was Dyno-Rod that discovered suspicious flesh-like remains in them. The police were called and Nilsen confessed to his crimes. In total, he owned up to fifteen murders. The names of some of his victims remain unknown to this day.

At his trial, Nilsen tried to plead manslaughter on grounds of diminished responsibility, but was found guilty of murder and given a minimum sentence of twenty-five years, later increased to a whole-life tariff by the Home Secretary. Part of his time in the maximum security prison he spends in litigation. In 2001 he claimed that the governor's refusal to allow him access to gay pornography was a breach of his human rights, and in 2003 he challenged the authorities' refusal to allow him to publish his autobiography, *The History of a Drowning Boy*. In the end, his case did get into print, courtesy of a book written by Nilsen's long-term friend and collaborator, Matthew Malekos.

5

Gone But Not Forgotten

Here are some of the famous people who passed away in the 1970s. In order of their departure:

Bertrand Russell, 3rd Earl Russell
(18 May 1872–2 February 1970)
Mathematician, philosopher and peace campaigner. Awarded the Nobel Prize for Literature in 1950.

Hugh Dowding, 1st Baron Dowding
(24 April 1882–15 February 1970)
A Scot, who joined the Royal Flying Corps in 1914 and rose to become head of Fighter Command during the Battle of Britain. Created a peer in 1943.

E.M. (Edward Morgan) Forster
(1 January 1879–7 June 1970)
Novelist. Author of, among other things, *A Room with a View*, *Howards End* and *A Passage to India*. Collaborated with Benjamin Britten on the libretto of his opera *Billy Budd*.

Sir Allen Lane

(21 September 1902–7 July 1970)

Founder (in 1935) and publisher of Penguin Books, which revolutionised the publishing trade.

Iain MacLeod

(11 November 1913–20 July 1970)

Elected to Parliament as a Conservative in 1950. Made Chancellor of the Exchequer in 1970 and died a month later.

Sir John Barbirolli

(2 December 1899–29 July 1970)

Conductor, London-born but of Franco-Italian origins, particularly known for his long association with Manchester's Halle Orchestra.

John Boyd Orr, 1st Baron Boyd-Orr

(23 December 1880–25 June 1971)

A Scot, studied medicine and founded an institute to advance our understanding of nutrition. He was behind much of the government's food policy that kept the nation well nourished in the Second World War. Winner of the Nobel Peace Prize in 1949.

Cecil Day-Lewis

(27 April 1904–22 May 1972)

Irish-born poet (Poet Laureate 1968–72) and (as Nicholas Blake) detective story writer. Father of actor Daniel.

Duke of Windsor

(23 June 1894–28 May 1972)

One-time King Edward VIII, enthroned in January 1936, but abdicated in December 1936 in order to marry American divorcee Wallace Simpson.

Sir Francis Chichester
(17 September 1901–26 August 1972)
Long-distance yachtsman, who won the first solo transatlantic yacht race in 1960 and later made a successful solo voyage around the world.

Sir Compton Mackenzie
(17 January 1883–30 November 1972)
Writer and founder of *The Gramophone* magazine. Author of many works, he may best be remembered for *Whisky Galore* (and its filmed offshoot).

Charles Atlas
(30 October 1893–23 December 1972)
Born Angelo Siciliano. His family emigrated to America in 1904. A weakling in his youth, he developed a system of exercises to improve his physique. He legally changed his name and marketed the technique worldwide.

Elizabeth Bowen
(7 June 1899–22 February 1973)
Irish-born writer. Author of many works, the best known of which are *The Death of the Heart* and *The Heat of the Day.*

Sir Noel Coward
(16 December 1899–26 March 1973)
Playwright, songwriter, actor and entertainer. Many stage successes, including *Hay Fever*, *Private Lives*, *Blithe Spirit* and *This Happy Band*. Also wrote operettas and revues, and was famous as a witty and satirical cabaret performer.

Jack Hawkins

(14 September 1910–18 July 1973)

London-born film and stage actor, famous both for acclaimed Shakespeare performances and for screen appearances. Served as a colonel in the Second World War and later played 'stiff upper lip' characters in films such as *Bridge on the River Kwai* and *Lawrence of Arabia*.

J.R.R. (John Ronald Reuel) Tolkien

(3 January 1892–2 September 1973)

South African-born academic who became a professor of Anglo-Saxon at Oxford University. Author of *The Hobbit* and *Lord of the Rings*, adventures set in a world of his own invention.

W.H. (Wystan Hugh) Auden

(21 February 1907–28 September 1973)

Poet and supporter of left-wing causes. Married Erica Mann (daughter of author Thomas) to provide her with a passport out of Nazi Germany. An influential poet, whose poem 'Stop All the Clocks' (or 'Funeral Blues') became one of the nation's favourites after featuring in the film *Four Weddings and a Funeral*.

H.E. (Herbert Ernest) Bates

(16 May 1905–29 January 1974)

Novelist and playwright. Best known for *Fair Stood the Wind for France*, *The Jacaranda Tree* and *The Darling Buds of May*, the latter being the first in a series of books featuring the Larkin family.

Henry, Duke of Gloucester

(31 March 1900–10 June 1974)

Third son of George V

Sir James Chadwick

(20 October 1891–24 July 1974)

Physicist, discoverer of the neutron. Nobel Prize winner for physics in 1935. Worked on the Manhattan Project that developed the atomic bomb during the Second World War.

Bernard Fitzalan-Howard, 16th Duke of Norfolk

(30 May 1908–31 January 1975)

Senior royal in a noble family line going back to Roger Bigod (died 1107). Earl Marshal of England and, as such, took leading responsibility for organising the 1953 coronation of Elizabeth II.

Sir P.G. (Pelham Grenville) Wodehouse

(15 October 1881–14 February 1975)

Novelist. Much-loved creator of the Jeeves and Blandings series of novels. Briefly alienated from the British public, due to a series of German-controlled broadcasts he innocently made whilst interned during the Second World War.

Sir Arthur Bliss

(2 September 1891–27 March 1975)

Composer (including film music among his commissions), music director at the BBC (1942–44) and Master of the Queen's Musick (with a k) since 1953

Dame Barbara Hepworth

(10 January 1903–20 May 1975)

Sculptor. Died in a fire at her Cornwall studio.

Haile Selassie

(23 July 1891–27 August 1975)

Deposed Emperor of Ethiopia, exiled to England after the Italian conquest of what was then Abyssinia, and again in a domestic coup in 1974. Much loved by Rastafarians.

Eamon de Valera

(14 October 1882–29 August 1975)

Leading light in Ireland's struggle for independence. Three times prime minister of the Irish Republic and its president from 1959 to 1973.

Cardinal John Heenan

(26 January 1905–7 November 1975)

Known in the Second World War as the 'radio priest'. Roman Catholic Archbishop of Westminster and campaigner for reconciliation between religions.

Ross McWhirter

(12 August 1925–27 November 1975)

Journalist, Conservative activist and (from 1955) co-compiler of *The Guinness Book of Records*, shot dead at his London home by an IRA gunman, shortly after offering a £50,000 reward for the arrest of the IRA's London cell.

Dame Agatha Christie

(15 September 1890–12 January 1976)

Novelist, author of detective fiction including the Poirot and Miss Marple series. Also wrote under the name of Mary Westmacott.

L.S. (Laurence Stephen) Lowrie
(1 November 1887–23 February 1976)
Manchester-born and based painter, who specialised in
Lancashire industrial scenes populated by matchstick figures.

Bernard Montgomery, 1st Viscount Montgomery of Alamein
(17 November 1887–24 March 1976)
Wartime army field marshal, leader of the Eighth Army in North
Africa and commander of ground forces for the D-Day invasion.
Accepted the German surrender at the end of the war.

Dame Sybil Thorndyke
(24 October 1882–9 June 1976)
Trained as a pianist but became an actress. Among the parts
she played was the first British portrayal of St Joan, in Bernard
Shaw's play of that name.

Sir Mortimer Wheeler
(10 September 1890–22 July 1976)
Archaeologist who did much to popularise the subject.

Roy Thomson, 1st Baron Thomson of Fleet
(5 June 1894–4 August 1976)
Canadian-born proprietor of newspapers, including (from 1966)
The Times. From 1957, owner of Scottish Television, which he
famously described as 'a licence to print money', and a North
Sea oil explorer. Made a baron in 1964 'for public services'.

Percy Shaw
(15 April 1890–1 September 1976)
Yorkshire-born inventor of 'cat's eyes' in 1934. The wartime
blackout gave a huge boost to their sales and he was given an
OBE for services to exports in 1965.

Dame Edith Evans

(8 February 1888–October 14 1976)

Actress, known for a variety of roles, most famously as Lady
Bracknell in *The Importance of Being Earnest* (filmed in 1952).

Deryck Cooke

(14 September 1919–26 October 1976)

From a poor working-class background, he was the composer,
musicologist and broadcaster who completed Mahler's *Symphony
No. 10* (first performance 1964, revised version published 1975).
Worked for the BBC almost all his life. Later years marred by
ill-health.

Sir Basil Spence

(13 August 1907–19 November 1976)

Probably the leading British architect of the immediate post-war
period, his commissions included pavilions for the Festival of
Britain, the British Embassy in Rome and additions to many
British universities, but he is perhaps best known for Coventry
Cathedral.

Baron Benjamin Britten

(22 November 1913–4 December 1976)

Composer of a variety of chamber, orchestral and choral music,
and several important operas, such as *Peter Grimes*, *Billy Budd*
and *Gloriana*. Also an accomplished pianist, often accompanying
singer Peter Pears. Co-founder of the Aldeburgh Festival.

Anthony Eden, 1st Earl of Avon

(12 June 1897–14 January 1977)

Former Conservative prime minister (1955–57). Became an MP
in 1923 and served in the shadow of Winston Churchill from
1940 onwards. Ordered the Suez occupation in 1956, which
ended in a debacle. Resigned on health grounds.

Anthony Crosland

(29 August 1918–19 February 1977)

Labour politician, holding several government posts under
Harold Wilson. Unsuccessful bidder for the party leadership in
1976. Influential as a moderniser of the party.

Brian Faulkner, Baron Faulkner of Downpatrick

(18 February 1921–3 March 1977)

Former Northern Ireland politician, and its sixth and last prime
minister. His political career started as the then-youngest-ever
member of the Northern Irish Parliament. He was made a baron
a matter of days before his death in a hunting accident.

Henry Williamson

(1 December 1895–13 August 1977)

Writer, best known for his nature stories such as *Tarka the Otter*,
The Peregrine's Saga and *Salar the Salmon*, and for his support for
Oswald Mosley and Hitler.

Leopold Stokowski

(18 April 1882–13 September 1977)

London-born orchestral conductor of Polish and Irish origins.
Attended the Royal College of Music, aged 13. Made his
conducting debut in 1912 and was still doing so in 1977, aged
95. Best known to the general public for the soundtrack to Walt
Disney's *Fantasia*.

'Bing' (Harry Lillis) Crosby

(3 May 1904–14 October 1977)

Singer and actor. Sold 500 million records, including 30 million copies of 'White Christmas'. Made a series of successful *Road to...* films with Bob Hope.

Sir Michael Balcon

(19 May 1896–17 October 1977)

Film producer, founder of Gainsborough Pictures and head of production at Ealing Studios. Gave Alfred Hitchcock his first directing job. Responsible for many classic British films.

Richard Addinsell

(13 January 1904–14 November 1977)

Composer, among other things, of the *Warsaw Concerto*, written for the 1941 film *Dangerous Moonlight*. It was written 'in the style of Rachmaninoff', after the man himself refused to provide music for the film.

Sir Terence Rattigan

(10 June 1911–30 November 1977)

British playwright and screenwriter. His plays encompassed comedy (*French Without Tears*) and dramas (*The Winslow Boy*, *The Browning Version* and *The Deep Blue Sea*). He also did film adaptations of his own and others' works. He was at one stage the world's highest-paid screenwriter.

Clementine Ogilvy Spencer-Churchill, Baroness Spencer-Churchill
(1 April 1885–12 December 1977)
Widow of Sir Winston and a peeress in her own right (she
was made Baroness Spencer-Churchill in 1965 and sat as a
cross-bencher). They married in 1908 – a union that would last
fifty-six years and produce five children.

Sir Charles ('Charlie') Chaplin
(16 April 1889–25 December 1977)
Film actor and director. Born in London, the son of music-hall
performers. Joined Karno's vaudeville troupe before going to
Hollywood in 1914, where his 'little tramp' character became
a great hit. Did not enter the world of sound movies until 1940,
where his leading role in *The Great Dictator* won him his only
Oscar nomination.

Joe Davis

(15 April 1904–10 July 1978)

Possibly the world's greatest ever snooker player, undefeated between 1927 and 1946.

Georgi Markov

(1 March 1929–15 September 1978)

Bulgarian dissident writer. Defected to the West in 1968, where he worked for the BBC World Service and other broadcasters. Murdered by being stabbed with a poisoned umbrella (thought to be the work of the Bulgarian secret police).

Airey Neave

(23 January 1916–30 March 1979)

First British escapee from Colditz POW camp in the Second World War. Highly decorated for his war service. Conservative MP from 1951. Prominent among the group that deposed Edward Heath in favour of Margaret Thatcher. Blown up by Irish republicans in the car park of the Houses of Parliament.

Nicholas Monsarrat

(22 March 1910–8 August 1979)

Author of, among other things, *The Cruel Sea*, based on his Second World War naval experiences, and *The Tribe that Lost its Head*.

Louis Mountbatten, 1st Earl Mountbatten of Burma

(25 June 1900–27 August 1979)

Naval officer and diplomat, his positions included Supreme Allied Commander South East Asia (1943–45), the last Viceroy of India (1947), First Sea Lord (1955–59) and Chief of Defence Staff (1959–65). Closely related to the Royal Family, he was assassinated when his boat was blown up by the IRA.

Dame Gracie Fields

(9 January 1898–27 September 1979)

Singer, actress. Born in Rochdale, her long career encompassed
music hall, radio, television and films. Created a dame in 1978.

Sir Barnes Wallace

(26 September 1887–30 October 1979)

Aeronautical engineer and inventor of, among other things,
the R100 airship (1929), the 'dambuster' bouncing bomb,
the geodetic structure – widely used, including in the structure
of the Second World War Wellington bomber – and the first
variable-geometry (swing-wing) aircraft of the 1950s.

Joyce Grenfell

(10 February 1910–30 November 1979)

Actress, singer/songwriter, purveyor of comic monologues,
often mocking the English middle classes.

6

Power to the People

Trade Union Power

The 1970s marked the high point of trade union power in Britain. Union membership peaked at over 13.2 million in 1979 – 53 per cent of the workforce. By 1990 it had fallen to below 10 million and today is less than 6 million. But during the 1970s unions were offered the chance to influence government policy to a degree that had not been seen before then (and certainly has not been seen since).

The power of the unions had long been a concern to both the political left and right. The 'one nation' Tories of the 1950s did not act upon their distaste for the unions, failing to detect a strong groundswell of public opinion in favour of such a measure at that time. It was the Labour government of the 1960s that first at least contemplated reducing the power of the unions. In 1968 it set up a royal commission into industrial relations. The following year saw the publication of *In Place of Strife*, a white paper drawn up in secret by the then Employment Secretary, Barbara Castle, helped by Prime Minister Harold Wilson. This would have required unions to hold a proper ballot before striking, and established an industrial board to enforce settlements in disputes, but it split the Cabinet when presented to them. Ironically, the opposition to it was led by

Jim Callaghan, whose time as prime minister would later be ended largely as a result of industrial disputes, which would probably have been illegal, had these proposals made it into law.

The 1970s began under a Conservative government led by Edward Heath, another 'liberal' one-nation Tory, who was (at least initially) sympathetic to both trade unionism and government intervention in the economy (as when he stepped in to nationalise and save the aircraft engine division of Rolls-Royce when it faced bankruptcy). By now, public unease was starting to grow about union power and 1971 saw an Industrial Relations Act pass into law, which minutely regulated trade union behaviour. It was hugely unpopular with the unions, which brought somewhere between 120,000 and 250,000 (depending on whose estimate you believed) 'kill the Bill' protesters out onto the streets. Even so, a 1972 survey suggested that half the population still thought the unions were too powerful; that figure was to rise to 60 per cent by 1974 and 70 per cent the following year.

Union power even made it into the hit parade. In February 1973 the Strawbs' single 'Part of the Union' reached Number 2 in the charts. Just a few phrases from the lyrics will give you the flavour: 'You won't get me I'm part of the union, till the day I die'; 'I always get my way if I strike for higher pay'; 'So though I'm a working man I can ruin the government's plan'.

The Oil Crisis of 1973

OPEC, the Organisation of the Petroleum Exporting Countries, was set up in 1960 to stop western industrialised nations driving down the price of crude oil, at the same time as they increased consumption by an average of 5 per cent a year. OPEC's main weapon was control over the rate of production. Things started to get more serious in 1971, when the United States disconnected the value of the dollar from that of gold, and any other nations whose currency was still tied to gold followed suit. Nations tried to boost their foreign reserves by printing money and the inevitable result was inflation. Oil prices, hitherto set in dollars, bought the oil-producing countries less and less of the west's manufactures and foodstuffs. As the Shah of Iran put it:

> You [western nations] increased the price of wheat you sell us by 300 per cent and the same for sugar and cement ... You buy our crude oil and sell it back to us, refined as petrochemicals, at a hundred times the price you paid us ... it's only fair that, from now on, you should pay more for oil. Let's say ten times more.

In fact, the OPEC price increase of 16 October 1973 was not ten times, but 70 per cent, to $5.11 a barrel. But at the same time, it announced a 5 per cent reduction in production, to be followed by a series of similar cuts until its political and economic objectives had been achieved. OPEC also responded by moving to oil prices based on gold. The big oil price increases of 1973 to 1974 just about got the OPEC members back to the income they had been receiving in the days of the gold-linked dollar. But their objectives were not just economic: they were also aimed at punishing the United States for its support of Israel in the Yom Kippur War of October 1973.

One impact of this was to fuel the inflation already present in western economies, and it drove up the price of coal, along with other forms of energy. Governments of all persuasions saw pay restraint as one of the means of controlling this inflation, and the Conservative government of the day introduced caps to pay in the public sector and encouraged the private sector to follow suit. Pay started to fall behind price increases, and one group that took a dim view of this was the mineworkers. From the 1960s their incomes had fallen behind other groups of workers. They had a big strike in 1972; they demanded 25 per cent, the Coal Board offered 7.5 per cent (which the miners swiftly turned down)

and they finally settled for 20 per cent plus other concessions. This blew a big hole in the government's proposed 8 per cent ceiling for wage settlements. Incidentally, the strike saw some of the first instances of mass picketing, including of premises which were not the strikers' place of work (secondary picketing). The laws on picketing were at this time rather vague, with strikers being allowed to choose just about anywhere to picket (except people's homes), using whatever forms of 'peaceful persuasion' they thought fit. This technique was being developed to its most 'persuasive' (if not necessarily 'peaceful') by Arthur Scargill and his Yorkshire mineworkers, and would become a big issue later in this decade and into the next.

However, the rest of the trade union movement was not prepared to see the miners treated as a special case, and a whole round of inflationary pay increases followed their example, which, by late 1973, had wiped out most of the gains that the miners had made in 1972. The miners responded by introducing a work to rule, banning overtime, with the threat of a strike to follow. The overtime ban alone reduced coal production by around a third. The nation depended upon the miners working overtime and coal reserves started to shrink as discussions between the miners and the Heath government failed to make progress.

The Three-Day Week

In late 1973, the government decided to eke out the remaining supplies of coal by introducing a three-day working week. Under this, commercial users of electricity (essential users were exempted) were only allowed to operate three consecutive days in the working week, and could not introduce extended working hours on those days. Other restrictions were introduced – for example, the television stations had to stop broadcasting at 10.30 p.m., there was no floodlit sport and there was a blanket 50mph speed limit on all roads to save petrol. The restrictions took effect from the start of 1974 and were to run until 7 March. On 5 February the miners voted for the overtime ban to escalate into an all-out strike. Two days later the government called a general election, using it to ask the country the question 'Who governs Britain?'

The answer to that question which came back through the ballot box perhaps summed up Britain in the 1970s – it was 'well, no one does, really'. For the Conservatives had the largest number of votes and Labour had the largest number of seats, without either one having an overall majority in Parliament. Eventually, Labour put together a minority administration, which struggled on until a further election in October gave them at least a narrow working majority. Perhaps a more significant guide to public opinion as to who governed Britain came in another survey, which asked: 'Who is the most powerful man in Britain?' One in four said the prime minister, but twice that number named Jack Jones, the head of the Transport and General Workers' Union. One election graffito read, 'Vote Jack Jones, cut out the middle man.'

The Social Contract

In the wake of Heath's failures on the industrial relations front, the new Labour government looked for a radically new approach. Naturally enough, it turned to an idea that had its roots in ancient Buddhist teaching, in Plato's *Republic* and, perhaps most famously, in a 1762 work by Jean-Jacques Rousseau. The social contract says that, in its 'state of nature', man's life is (to quote another political thinker, Thomas Hobbes) 'solitary, poor, nasty, brutish and short'. The strong take what they want from, and do what they like to, those weaker than themselves. Therefore individuals voluntarily agree to surrender some of their freedoms to a government, in return for their remaining liberties being protected. In Rousseau's model of the social contract, it would not be an absolute monarch who had the divine right to make laws: only the people as a whole had that right. This was radical thinking for 1762, but how did it relate to 1970s Britain?

Many people in the early 1970s thought that Britain's informal social contract was breaking down, and that we were reverting to a state of nature in which the strong (in particular, the unions) were pursuing a beggar-my-neighbour policy that impoverished weaker groups in society. Labour's big idea was to get the unions to sign up afresh to a new social contract. The deal was that, in return for the repeal of the Conservatives' much-hated 1971 Industrial Relations Act, plus food subsidies and a freeze on rent increases, the Trades Union Congress would persuade its members to co-operate in a policy of voluntary wage restraint. By bringing them into the tent of government and making concessions to them, the unions would hopefully be persuaded to be more responsible and see the bigger picture of the national good. After all, this kind of arrangement worked perfectly well in Scandinavia and other European countries.

Some saw the unions as a bunch of wild-eyed, left-wing ideologues, hell-bent on imposing a communist dictatorship. But that was far from the truth, certainly as far as the rank-and-file membership of the unions was concerned. A good number of them would be among those who voted Margaret Thatcher into power at the end of the decade. Their interest was simply in the size of their take-home pay. As Dominic Sandbrook put it, they didn't want a new Jerusalem, they wanted a new Cortina.

And this was the problem with the social contract. Even if the union leadership wanted to act in a statesmanlike manner (and they were often competing with each other for membership, and so did not want to be the first to be seen advocating wage restraint), they did not have the power over their members to deliver it (that infernal democracy again). Hence the unions were happy to discuss the concessions the government would give them, but mention wage restraint and the shutters came down. At one meeting, Jack Jones made it clear that it would be disastrous if word got out that they had even been discussing prices and incomes policy. Nor did the union leaders necessarily see statesmanship as part of their remit. As miners' leader Joe Gormley said, 'Our role in society is to look after our members, not run the country.'

For their part, the government more than delivered on its promises to the unions. Major improvements to people's working conditions were introduced, through the Health and Safety at Work Act, the Trades Unions and Labour Relations Act, the Employment Protection Act, the Sex Discrimination Act and the Trades Unions and Labour Relations Amendment Act, as well as setting up the Advisory Conciliation and Arbitration Service (ACAS), delivering the food and rent subsidies, pension increases and price restrictions.

In return, the unions followed one after the other in making ever greater pay demands. In the public sector, teachers, nurses and postmen all got generous settlements; Ford workers got 37 per cent, just seven months after their last settlement, and BBC employees 28 per cent. Wage inflation was nearing 20 per cent and the balance-of-payments deficit and government borrowing were both at record levels. Before long, all but its most fanatical adherents began to realise that the social contract was not working – and could not work. But its credibility survived long enough for Labour to use the social contract as shorthand for industrial peace in the autumn 1974 general election.

Grunwick

One dispute would come to epitomise the decade's battle between left and right. Grunwick was a photographic processing laboratory in north-west London, in the days when cameras still used film. It was run by an Anglo-Indian named George Ward, who was noted for his ferocious discipline of the staff (and for relatively low pay). He employed mostly Asian women, and there was no room for dissent, let alone trade unionism, in his organisation. There was compulsory overtime during the peak summer months, during which staff could not take holiday. They even had to ask permission to go to the toilet. The dispute began in the heat wave of the summer of 1976, when a number of employees were sacked after refusing to take on even more additional work in their sweltering workplace. They sought the help of the Brent Trades Council, and local official Jack Dromey (a future deputy general secretary of the Transport and General Workers' Union and a Labour shadow minister in Parliament) rallied to their cause. For their part, the National Association for Freedom lined up firmly behind the employer, who, they said, was providing jobs in an area where they were badly needed.

At first the picketing of the premises was low-key and relatively ineffectual. A sizeable proportion of the workforce remained in work. The dispute dragged on until June 1977, when Dromey decided to escalate it. A nationwide call went out for a mass picket and, on 13 June, several hundred people, representing a variety of left-wing interests, turned up. Also present in numbers – estimated at 300 – were the police. Accounts differ as to who started it, but fighting broke out and by the end of the morning eighty-four protesters had been arrested. There were complaints that the police had used excessive violence in making their arrests, many of which were of women. Part of the police presence consisted of the Special Patrol Group (SPG), who were brought in to supplement beleaguered local forces and who were renowned for their 'robust' handling of protesters. For their part, the police complained of violence by the demonstrators.

The escalation continued. In June and July, it was estimated that 18,000 demonstrators came up against 3,500 policemen; 297 people were arrested and ninety-seven policemen injured. Grunwick was now front-page news, and being seen at the picket line (and better still, getting arrested) was regarded as de rigueur for any prominent person of the left-wing persuasion – Sandbrook called it the 'Ascot of the left'. Miners' leader Arthur Scargill turned up with 150 miners and was given the undivided attention of both the television cameras and the SPG as he was duly arrested. But the image that really caught the public's eye was that of a police constable, a member of the SPG, lying unconscious on the pavement with blood pouring from his head. Even some of the pickets were at pains to condemn violence on this scale, which served only to detract from the strikers' case.

Henceforth, things started to go the employer's way. A poll commissioned by Ward established that the vast majority of Grunwick's remaining workforce did not want a trade union and did not even want their striking former colleagues reinstated. (Ward took the precaution of giving his remaining staff a

15 per cent pay rise before sending in the pollsters, who apparently did not observe the strictest confidentiality in gathering the employees' 'views'.) An attempt by postal workers to bring down Grunwick by boycotting its mail deliveries (84 per cent of its business was mail order) was thwarted, partly in the courts and partly by its supporters through covert action in smuggling out the company's mail. The rainbow coalition of pickets began to fall out with each other and lose heart. The campaign dragged on until July 1978, when the picket was formally withdrawn.

The campaign had been a propaganda gift to the right-wing press and politicians, who used it as evidence of how far a Labour-governed Britain had moved towards authoritarian mob rule. It helped pave the way for the clampdown on industrial disputes under future Conservative administrations. For their part, the left took some small comfort from the evidence it gave of working-class solidarity transcending race and gender, with miners coming to the aid of Asian women workers.

The Winter of Discontent

Things were looking up for Labour by the autumn of 1978. The more centrist government of Jim Callaghan seemed to be making some progress in getting the economy under control and the opinion polls suggested that there was a good chance of it being returned for a second term in the forthcoming general election. Almost everyone assumed that Labour would go to the country that same autumn but Callaghan decided to wait until the spring of 1979, allowing more time for the pendulum to swing further in his favour. (North Sea oil – seen as Britain's economic saviour – was just starting to come on-stream.) The delay turned out to be one of the biggest mistakes in British political history.

Labour was still trying to get the nation's crippling rate of inflation under control and, as part of this, introduced a policy of limiting pay increases to a guideline of 5 per cent.

This depended upon the unions exercising moderation in their demands but, like his predecessors, Callaghan failed to recognise that the union leadership had lost much of its power to control its membership at a local level. Those members were by and large not interested in moderation, if it meant missing out on their new three-piece suites and foreign holidays. They were not left-wing extremists but proto-Thatcherites. Few expected the guideline to work, so nobody was willing to moderate their wage demands at the risk of falling behind everybody else (this despite an opinion poll showing 69 per cent of trade unionists in favour of the 5 per cent limit – no doubt, for everybody else but themselves).

Ford was one of the first employers to break the guideline, settling a long strike with a 17 per cent pay increase, and others soon followed suit. Local authority manual workers, miners and NHS auxiliary workers all put in for 40 per cent, British Leyland manual workers for 30 per cent and bakery workers for 22 per cent. Tanker drivers topped the list with a massive 60 per cent claim, and the employers' response – 13 per cent, partly paid for by productivity improvements – meant that industrial action would soon follow. For its part, the government drew up secret plans for soldiers to drive the petrol tankers, with who knows what implications for industrial confrontation, let alone safety.

To add to the government's woes, the weather now took a hand, with some of the worst winter snows for more than half a century. All but three matches in the New Year's Day Football League programme had to be cancelled, as were postal services and milk deliveries. The AA advised people to stay off the roads (not that there was much petrol to be had) and the railways warned of 'severe delays'. Local authority gritter-lorry drivers were already on a work to rule. Vegetables – indeed groceries of all kinds – were in short supply and, worst of all, some pubs had the beer in their cellars freeze up. Prime Minister Callaghan responded by jetting off to the Caribbean for a pre-arranged major powers summit. Shivering Britons saw Callaghan looking out from their televisions and newspapers, smiling as he sunned himself on the beach. It did nothing for the government's case: 'Crisis? What Crisis?' and 'Wish we were there, Jim!' said the newspaper headlines.

Public-sector workers were no more willing than their private-sector counterparts to sacrifice themselves on the altar of pay moderation. Railway staff, water and sewage workers all took industrial action. Pickets at the docks and elsewhere took the law into their own hands, deciding what goods should be moved and on what terms. Nothing was sacred: food, essential industrial goods and even life-saving medical supplies could only be delivered on the pickets' say-so, and not even the most senior union management could influence them. The National Union of Public Employees demanded a 50 per cent increase for its members, many of whom were among the lowest paid workers, and even the nurses demanded an immediate 25 per cent. In January 1979 a group of unions called their members out for a 'day of action' (i.e. total inaction) in support of a minimum wage of £60 a week, in the biggest industrial action since the General Strike of 1926. Schools and public buildings were shut, buses were taken off the roads and hospitals turned away all but emergency cases. Volunteers had to provide emergency ambulance services, piles of uncollected rubbish grew ever higher and more verminous, and in some areas the dead could not be buried.

Still the government vacillated about declaring a state of emergency, something even Attlee's Labour government had done in response to the 1940s dock strikes. On Valentine's Day 1979 the government and the TUC signed a concordat, committing both sides to work towards a 5 per cent inflation target by the spring of 1982. Given the evidence of the TUC's patent inability to influence the actions of its membership, this was a joke and was seen as such by most of the public.

Sir Geoffrey Howe summed up the concordat as 'the same old cobblers'. The Conservatives at least were delighted with it, insofar as the Winter of Discontent had done what its protagonists had least wanted – it had alienated the union movement and what were seen as its fellow travellers in the Labour Party from mainstream public opinion. In a MORI poll in September 1978, 82 per cent of the public thought the unions wielded too much power. A further poll in 1983 showed that 82 per cent of the public favoured secret ballots for strikes, 69 per cent wanted restrictions on union closed shops and 88 per cent wanted ballots for the union leadership. The Winter of Discontent had more or less guaranteed a Conservative election victory, and gave them carte blanche to legislate robustly against union power, which they duly did throughout the 1980s. There would be compulsory strike ballots, a ban on flying pickets and secondary industrial action, an end to the closed shop and a variety of changes to the tax and benefit systems that made it much harder for the strikers and their families to support themselves during industrial action.

Jim Callaghan was in no doubt as to why Labour had lost the election: 'The unions did it: people could not forget and would not forgive what they had to suffer from the unions last winter.'

7

Child's Play: 1970s Toys

In this chapter, we will look at some of the toys children (and quite a few adults) were playing with in the 1970s, and the stories behind them.

Atari 2600 Games Console

Before it made the 2600, Atari had had a great hit in 1975 with *Pong*, an electronic table tennis game. For a time, its 2600 video game console, released in September 1977, was to dominate the video games market, to the extent that the name Atari became synonymous with video gaming. Rather than having non-microprocessor-dedicated hardware and built-in games, it had microprocessor-based hardware and ROM cartridges, which enabled a wide variety of games to be played on a single machine. This idea had originally been developed by Hewlett Packard for much more expensive office computers, but Warner Communications underwrote Atari's costs of about $100 million in developing it for the games market. Atari was not the first to bring out a cartridge-based console – it was beaten to it by Fairchild's Channel F and RCA's Studio 2, but Atari's was the one that seized the public imagination.

The original package consisted of the console, two joystick controllers, a conjoined pair of paddle controllers and a single cartridge game – initially *Combat*, but later *Pac-Man*. It seems to have taken the public a while to realise that it was possible to play any number of different games on it; only 250,000 were sold in 1977 and a more respectable 550,000 the following year, albeit out of a production run of 800,000. Atari was so far making a loss, which Warner again had to bankroll. But 1979 saw the product really take off. It was the top Christmas present of the year, selling a million units.

Its real zenith was to be in the early 1980s, starting in January 1980 when Atari launched its version of the hit arcade game *Space Invaders*. This doubled sales to 2 million and saw Atari's gross profit rise to over \$2 billion. By 1982, 10 million consoles had been sold. Atari was by now making a healthy profit; the console, which cost about \$40 to produce, was selling for an average of \$125 and a game cartridge, which cost \$4.50–6.00 to make and \$1–2 to promote, went for \$18.95 wholesale.

The flexibility of the machine made it possible for third parties to develop games for it. The first to do so were four breakaway Atari employees, who founded the company Activision and brought out four games that were superior to Atari's own. Atari tried and failed in the courts to stop them doing so. Whilst third-party product added much to the machine's appeal, it was not without its problems. One of the main ones was a lack of quality control. For example, a company called Mystique developed a series of pornographic games for it. One of these, *Custer's Revenge*, had the colonel raping a bound Native American woman. Not surprisingly, this attracted complaints from both women's and Native American groups, though anyone who could derive erotic gratification from the ridiculous Lego-like figures depicted in it was in serious need of help. Whether the game was erotic or not, Atari ended up suing the company.

The development of a third-party market was one of the factors leading to the great video game collapse of 1983–85. Industry revenues, which peaked at \$3.2 billion in 1983, fell by about 97 per cent to \$100 million in 1985. It almost killed off the entire industry and certainly did for Atari. In the absence of any control over the third-party market, it was flooded with poor quality games, which fatally undermined consumer confidence.

Atari was equally guilty. It rushed out *Pac-Man* for the Christmas market in 1982. This adaptation of the popular arcade game was universally panned, sales forecasts were over-estimated, and there were major cost overruns in its production and marketing. 'Not one aspect of the title went unruined,' said one reviewer. *ET the Extra-Terrestrial*, also rushed out after just six weeks' development, was described as one of the worst games ever seen. Its sales fell so far short of forecasts that thousands were allegedly sent straight to landfill in New Mexico. Retailers, swamped with choice, tried to return unsold products, but the 'garden shed' companies that manufactured many of them could offer neither refunds nor alternative products. To add to their problems, the market for the 2600 console had by now just about reached saturation point and the emergence of the home computer market, which could run games as well as performing other tasks, also hit sales. One company in particular, Commodore, went aggressively for the games market, offering a trade-in for the Atari against one of its computers.

The market only began to revive with the arrival of the Japanese Nintendo system. Nintendo learned from Atari's mistakes: it limited the number of titles produced and developed a seal of quality to weed out inferior ones. More to the point, it developed lock-out chips to prevent unauthorised products loading.

Star Wars Action Figures

In the 1970s, as now, model action figures were big business for the toy industry. The American market leader for these figures at the time was the Mego Corporation and, in 1976, it was offered the licence for action figures from a forthcoming science fiction film, being made on the cheap in England with largely unknown

American stars. They turned it down, and the decision proved to be something akin to the record producer who turned down the Beatles, for the film was *Star Wars*. The franchise went instead to a company called Kenner and, when the film came out in May 1977, Kenner was utterly unprepared for the tidal wave of demand for their product that followed. Unable to assemble enough stock for the key Christmas period, it hit upon a marketing plan of genius – it sold empty boxes!

The Early Bird Certificate Package consisted mainly of a box containing a certificate that could be sent to Kenner and exchanged for four *Star Wars* figures (when available). The range was soon expanded to include more figures and their vehicles, but in the run-up to Christmas 1978 demand still outstripped supply, giving rise to accusations that Kenner was in some way manipulating the market. Having said that, Kenner sold 40 million Star Wars products in 1978, turning over $100 million. The film sequels introduced new characters and new action-figure marketing opportunities, though some of these had their moments. The plan to market Boba Fett complete with a backpack carrying a real firing missile had to be abandoned, amid health and safety fears that the tiny tots would put each other's eyes out.

Demand only petered out in mid-1985, by which time Kenner had sold over 300 million *Star Wars* figures. Given this figure, it is difficult to believe that rarities exist but, in October 2013, a model of a character called Jawa sold for £10,200. It is thought to be one of only six known examples in the world.

More generally, the collectors' market for these figures can only be said to give anoraks a bad name. Minute differences in sculpting, accessories, paint detailing or sculpting materials can all affect the value of the item. Does your Luke Skywalker have a single- or a double-telescoping light sabre? Does your R2-D2 have an extendable 'sensorscope'? These things matter, apparently. A market has grown up in the forged upgrading of your model's accessories, to bring them up to a more desirable specification (something much frowned upon by purists). Even the unopened packaging in which your toy must sit (un-played with) counts. Was it related to the original *Star Wars* film, or to one of the sequels? There are currently fifty-seven different packaging combinations recognised (and, before you write to correct me, this does not include figures released through overseas companies or the *Droids* or *Ewoks* ranges). Overseas it gets even more complicated, with some of the European models marketed in 'trilogo' three-language packaging (which is in greater demand in certain benighted quarters, for some reason).

Kenner's success was rewarded by being taken over, first by Tonka in 1987 and then by Hasbro in 1991. The latter benefited from the reissue of the *Star Wars* trilogy on laserdisc and VHS, and it celebrated by issuing a new edition of the figures – in a more heroic style with bigger 'muscles'. They continue to be marketed to this day.

Action Man

In the 1960s the American company Hasbro produced G.I. Joe, an action figure celebrating the US armed forces. The sales manager of an English subsidiary, Palitoy, brought one back to England for his grandson and, seeing its reception, suggested to his management that they produce something similar. There were initial concerns about 'boys playing with dolls', but the d-word was soon banned and they came up with the name Action Man. This generic name enabled the d ... I mean figure ... to be associated with almost any kind of action, from military to exploration, sport and outer space.

From its launch, it was up against Pedigree Toys' Tommy Gunn. The company marketed the Cindy Doll and Tommy copied aspects of G.I. Joe but, despite its superiority in some respects, Palitoy was able to see it off by 1968. Other, more cheaply produced, alternatives also failed to make a dent in the market. From 1970,

Action Man developed with a number of identities and new features, including flocked hair, gripping hands and scary 'eagle eyes' that swivelled at the touch of a button. He also has a scar on his cheek, which has its own trademark protection. One, particularly British, variety was the 'Ceremonials' option, a package that included a Life Guards horse and full ceremonial regalia. One area of action that was ruled out for Action Man resulted from the understandable absence of any genitalia, though this was addressed in 1979 by the issue of moulded blue underpants to disguise any shortcoming in this department.

As with the Star Wars figures, collectors of Action Man have studied the changes to his anatomy with the kind of forensic detail normally reserved for murder victims. His height, foot size, coloration and softness of head have all been carefully documented. Even an extra line, introduced above his buttocks, is a matter of public record. Does the man have no privacy? He also suffers from the effects of ageing. Early models had rigid hands, modelled on G.I. Joe's, but having to glue the gun into the hands of your soldier was a major disadvantage for a fighting man. Flexible, gripping vinyl hands were introduced in 1973, though some of the early examples of them are now prone to discoloration and falling apart. The early models also had a moulded vinyl painted head which, over time, has been prone to shrinking and hardening.

There was a talking version from the late 1960s onwards, but Action Man was a person of few words. His vocabulary was limited to eight (in later versions just five) battlefield commands, which he uttered at random, depending upon how far you pulled out his string. None of them would have been a hit at dinner parties. But none of this mattered, for, in 1980, Action Man won the toy of the decade award. Finally, bad news for nationalists: Action Man, the all-British hero, is in fact oriental – Hong Kong being the place of birth (or, rather, manufacture) for many of his namesakes.

It will come as no surprise that Action Man has been accused of making those who played with him more inclined to be belligerent. In November 2013 it was announced that the Royal Holloway University was being given a £500,000 research budget for a two-year project, to find out whether this is indeed the case. The Ministry of Defence presumably must think it does, since it licenses its own range of Her Majesty's Armed Forces action figures. In an article in the *Daily Telegraph*, a passionate defender of Action Man argued that he was only part of a 1970s generation that focused on and, in many cases, could well remember the war. There were constantly war films on the television and in the cinema, and comics like *Victor* and *Valiant* that glorified the exploits of our own brave Tommies to their young readers, as they overcame the evil sausage-devouring Huns. Eat lead, Fritz!

Sindy

Sindy is a middle-aged woman now – she had her fiftieth birthday in 2013 and has had a tough life. She has been in a series of relationships with men who only wanted to make money out of her and her dreams of making it big in America came to nought. A victim of repeated cosmetic surgery, her body is now beginning to be marked by the ravages of time and she has disappeared entirely from the high streets of Britain. Obviously, her story extends a long way either side of the decade we are interested in but, given that she was Britain's best-selling toy in 1970, she merits a place on our pages. We will focus mainly on what happened to her up to the end of the 1970s.

In 1963, Pedigree, a long-established British doll manufacturer, decided to add a fashion doll to its range. The company was were offered a licence to manufacture Barbie, the American original, but its market research indicated that she was unpopular with British customers, so it decided to go it alone – well, not entirely alone, for Pedigree modelled its girl on a different, rather more homely American prototype called Tammy. Her name, Sindy, was chosen by a street poll of potential customers (with 'Cindy' being misspelt to help with the copyrighting.) Sindy was marketed in the 1960s as the 'free, swinging girl that every little girl wants to be' ... she has 'a dog, skates, a gramophone ... everything'.

Sure enough, Sindy, with her girl-next-door looks, proved more popular than Barbie in Britain. An entire circle of characters emerged around her. Boyfriend Paul appeared in 1965, younger sister Patch (Patch?) the following year, with friends Vicki and Mitzi, and Patch's friends Poppet and Betsy, all arriving in 1968. But the real money was in the accessories, which made up 70 per cent of the turnover. Much of it was clothes and shoes but, for a 'free, swinging girl' there seemed to be a good deal of domestic drudgery involved, with ranges including ironing boards, kitchen sinks and cookers that simulated the sound of sizzling bacon.

Through the 1970s Pedigree focused on turning out more and more of the money-spinning accessories, neglecting its advertising and market research. Sindy was in danger of her homely image becoming old-fashioned. At the end of the decade, Pedigree's attempt to launch Sindy on the American market failed; its American partner went into receivership. Attempts to resculpt Sindy to look more like Barbie ended up with both a drop in sales and legal action for breach of copyright by Barbie's owners, and further cosmetic surgery became necessary. There were yet more makeovers in the 1990s, as she passed from one ownership to another (five companies have so far manufactured her). As the years went on, some of the older models started showing their age. Melt marks began to appear at the shoulders and hips, the result of chemical reactions between the hard plastic torsos and the soft vinyl limbs.

But, for all her ups and downs, Sindy is highly collectable. The right model (a first-edition Sindy, complete with the original Foale and Tuffin 'weekenders' outfit, for example) can be worth £160–200. Rare friends of Sindy, like Mitzi, can command up to £500. As with the male collectors of Action Man, devotees of Sindy spend hours documenting minute differences in the various models, right down to whether a particular dress has a paper or a fabric label.

Just in case you are thinking that Barbie might be a good role model for young girls, scientists with too much time on their hands have warned that her dimensions, scaled up to full size, show her to be seriously underweight, and that she would have insufficient body fat to be healthy. She is an unsuitable companion in other ways. There is a talking variety of Barbie, whose conversation includes such subversive (to men) phrases as, 'I love shopping!' and 'Will we ever have enough clothes?', along with calls to go and eat pizza. Unsurprisingly, she is banned in Saudi Arabia, for her revealing clothes and shameful postures (though the latter are only at the whim of her owner).

Dungeons and Dragons

Dungeons and Dragons first saw the light of day (or should that be the gloom of an other-worldly twilight?) in 1974. It was the prototype for role-playing games. In a conventional wargame, the player would be in charge of an entire army. In D&D each player has just a single character, who goes on an imaginary adventure in a fantasy world. The game has a referee/storyteller – the dungeon master, who also plays the role of the inhabitants of this other world. The other characters interact with each other and with the inhabitants to solve problems, fight battles, collect treasure and gather knowledge. In this process, they can earn experience points that make them more powerful.

By the early 1980s, the game already had over 3 million devotees. To date, some 20 million people are said to have played D&D and the market for related books and equipment has so far been worth $1 billion. Many role-playing games have appeared since, but D&D remains the best known. It has variously won awards and been (so far falsely) linked to dark practices like Satanism and suicide. The space available in a little book does not allow me even to begin explaining the rules of the game (always assuming I understood them) but a few principles may help give a flavour.

The raw materials for playing the game are dice, the rule-books, a character sheet for each player (to which I will return), a gridded surface on which to play and miniature figures or markers to represent the players. Aside from playing, a major activity for gamers appears to be painting the miniature figures used in the game in exquisite and almost imperceptible detail. The dungeon master's role in the game is central. He (I say 'he' – it does sound like more of a male thing, though I will no doubt be corrected) decides such things as what the fantasy world's other inhabitants are like and what the outcomes of interactions between the leading characters and these inhabitants are. There are copious books of rules to help him make these decisions, though he apparently has godlike powers to depart from those rules, should he wish.

At the start of the game, each player creates his character's character, scoring them for things like strength, constitution, dexterity, intelligence, wisdom and charisma. He must also be given a racial identity (e.g. elf – or pixie?), an occupation (e.g. wizard – or perhaps chartered accountant?), ethical and moral positions and various powers and skills. As the game progresses, players say what their character intends to do, and the effect of their action is determined by a combination of the dungeon master's judgement, the rolling of dice and their character's ability scores and skills. Each game consists of an adventure, which the dungeon master can either make up or select from a book of pre-made adventures. The published ones include a background story, illustrations, maps and objectives. Who, for example, could resist the challenge of *Catacombs*?: 'Friar Renau's niece, Marguerite, has disappeared inside the catacombs. As ever more go missing, the Archbishop of the Silver Flame enlists your aid to find out why, and purge the crypts of insidious undead.'

Especially if you went equipped with: 'Grave wrappings for unarmed combat that can drain the life from your opponent and grant it to you as temporary hitpoints' or 'Drow smoke goggles which allow you to see your opponent's weaknesses and deliver deadly strikes'.

For some inexplicable reason, the game appears to have attracted a reputation for geekdom, and has been the butt of much humour and even satirical films. More seriously, it has been accused (mainly by Christian groups) of association with devil worship, witchcraft, suicide, murder and the portrayal of female humanoids with their busty substance on display. One player, a Chris Pritchard, was convicted in 1990 of murdering his stepfather, but a claimed link between the game and the crime has not been proven.

The Six Million Dollar Man and the Bionic Woman

'Steve Austin – astronaut. A man barely alive. We can rebuild him. We have the technology. We can make him better than he was before. Better – stronger – faster.'

Steve Austin was a test pilot, nearly killed when his craft crashed. He was rebuilt by the OSI (the Office of Scientific Intelligence – other definitions of the acronym are available) using nuclear-powered bionic spare parts (costing $6 million) that give him superhuman powers and his name. He is then sent out into the world to fight injustice wherever he encounters it. His first incarnation was in the novel *Cyborg* by Martin Caidin, but his real claims to fame were the television series and TV films starring Lee Majors that ran in the mid-1970s. Inevitably there had to be an action figure to accompany it, and this first appeared in 1975. Its features included:

- A bionic eye that the user could look through (apparently it did not work – some said it made things look further away, rather than magnifying them)
- An arm that could lift heavy objects simply by pressing a lever in his back – a car engine block was provided to demonstrate its awesome power
- Roll-back skin, to display some of his bionic components (this very quickly used to perish, go rigid and fall off – collectors can now purchase an improved nylon replacement)
- Later models had a bionic 'gripping' hand. For a time, they also had small removable bionic parts, until it was discovered that small children used to enjoy eating them
- There was also a full range of accessories – clothing, transport, a mission control centre, not to mention playmates in the form of his boss Oscar Goldman with his exploding briefcase (it didn't really – it just looked as though it had) and his

nemesis, the evil Maskatron (a master of disguise – he had three disguises, stored in a cavity in his chest)

There was also his feminine counterpart, the Bionic Woman – Lindsay Wagner in the television series, launched in 1976. In the series, Wagner plays Jaime Sommers, a top tennis professional and love interest for the bionic man – he proposes marriage at one stage. She suffers a near-fatal skydiving accident, but the bionic man persuades his employers to rebuild her as his feminine counterpart. The action figure's range of accessories did not exactly mark her out as an icon of feminism (or, indeed, action), including as they did platform shoes and a 'mission purse' containing a hairbrush, comb, 'make-up' and mirror, alongside her secret maps and code-breaking sheet. She did, however, have a bionic ear (that made a pinging noise), a preternaturally strong right arm and a running speed in excess of 60mph. Her bionic pet Alsatian dog, Maximillion (the million-dollar dog – get it?) has a turbo-charged jaw and a 90mph running speed. The Bionic Woman also has her evil opponents, the fembots. In the last series her love interest changes because the bionic man is unfaithful to her (he moves to a different television channel and is no longer contractually available for romance).

Spirograph

Spirograph started life as a technique designed by a mathematician, Bruno Abakanowicz, for measuring the area of a space defined by curves back in the late nineteenth century. A British engineer, Denys Fisher, developed it as a game in 1965. It consists of different sized flat plastic rings with gear teeth inside and out and holes for a pen to fit in and make tracings on a sheet of paper placed beneath them. But I am insulting your intelligence with this childish explanation; you will be wanting the full adult version. It is, of course, a device for producing mathematical roulette curves of the type technically known as hypotrochoids and epitrochoids. The mathematical basis is too simple (just 2–3 pages) to require detailed elaboration, except to remind you that the trajectory equations take the form:

$$X(t) = R[(1 - k) \cos t + lk \cos ((1 - k)/k) \times t] \text{ and}$$
$$Y(t) = R[(1 - k) \sin t + lk \sin ((1 - k)/k) \times t]$$

Like I said, it is a drawing game and, if you want to know more, feel free to ask someone else.

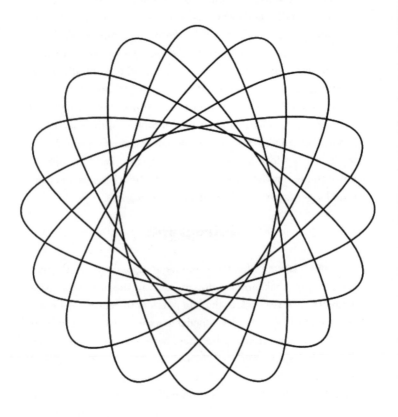

Play-Doh

Now this I understand. In the 1930s a man named Noah McVicker produced a product that removed the residues from coal fires from wallpaper. After the war, as the use of coal fires declined, so did the company's profits. Noah's nephew, Joe McVicker, was brought into the company to try and turn it around. He noticed that some nurseries were using the product to make models, since working with real modelling clay was rather tough on small fingers. McVicker made some changes to the recipe (such as adding colour, a scent that is supposed to smell of childhood – whatever that smells like – and reducing the salt content) and Play-Doh was launched in 1956. At first, it was available in four colours – red, blue, yellow and the original wallpaper-cleaner white. Now you can have virtually any colour you want, including glitter and glow-in-the-dark varieties.

It was an instant hit, making McVicker a millionaire before his twenty-seventh birthday. By 2005, 2 billion tubs, with a combined weight equal to 2,000 Statues of Liberty, had been sold, along with a lot of accessories. Many of these accessories seem to be devoted to turning the dough into lookalike food. What if the tiny tots eat it? Whilst it is not actually toxic, some of the ingredients seem unwholesome to adult eyes, including boric acid and a petroleum additive. The bulk of it consists of water, salt and flour. There are various homespun recipes for making it yourself, including at least one, involving peanut butter, that is intended to be edible.

Perhaps the oddest fact about the product is that 16 September is National Play-Doh Day. It must be true, because Hallmark cards say it is.

8

Sporting Heroes and Zeros

In this chapter we look at some of the high and low points of British sporting endeavour in the 1970s.

Formula 1

Let's get the facts out of the way first, so we can get onto the more interesting bits about the personalities. The 1970s were something of a golden age for British motor racing (following the even more golden age of the 1960s, where Britons won no fewer than six world championships). For three of the ten years of the 1970s we had a British world champion driver – Jackie Stewart in 1971 and 1973, and James Hunt in 1976 – and for no fewer than seven years out of ten the winning team was British. Lotus took three championships (1970, 1972 and 1978) with Tyrrell (1971 and 1973) and McLaren (1974 and 1976) winning two each. Only Ferrari prevented the British teams having a clean sweep. One engine dominated the decade, and beyond – the British-developed Cosworth Ford DFV, which powered all of the championship-winning cars except the Ferraris. This engine won 155 of the 262 Grands Prix in which it competed between 1967 and 1985, and in 1969 and 1973 won every single race in the championship.

Now for the personalities, and our 1970s world champions could not have been a more contrasting pair.

Safety Fast — Jackie Stewart

John Young Stewart (better known as Jackie) was born in 1939, the son of a successful Scottish car dealer and racing motorcyclist. In addition, his brother was also a racing driver, one highlight of whose career was skidding off during a wet British Grand Prix in 1953. Jackie was dyslexic and left school at 16 to work in his father's garage. He proved to be a crack shot with a rifle, winning national and European titles and almost representing Britain in the 1960 Olympics. But he found his true vocation when one of his father's customers gave Jackie a trial racing a sports car. He proved to be so good at it that he was upgraded to a full-race E-Type Jaguar, in which he promptly equalled the times set by established Grand Prix driver Roy Salvadori. Continued success earned him a test with the Tyrrell Formula 3 team, where he outpaced another Formula 1 legend, Bruce McLaren.

After turning down Formula 1 drives with Cooper and Lotus, he finally signed for BRM in 1965, coming third in his first season.

He won his first world championship in 1969, on his way to a total of twenty-seven Grand Prix wins, a record which stood until 1987. Among other achievements, he very nearly won the Indianapolis 500 race at his first attempt and was only prevented from co-driving with Steve McQueen in the Le Mans twenty-four-hour race by the fact that McQueen could not get insurance. Stewart retired slightly earlier than planned, after the death of his team mate François Cevert.

Today, Stewart is almost as famous for his championing of the cause of safety in Formula 1 as for his success in competition. The issue was brought rather forcibly to his attention during the 1966 Belgian Grand Prix. In those days, Formula 1 was a desperately dangerous business. A driver competing for five years stood a two-in-three chance of being killed. The events of that particular afternoon would be comical, had they not been so appallingly life-threatening. It rained on the first lap of the Grand Prix and Stewart's car left the track at 165mph. After hitting several objects, he found himself trapped in the car, upside down, with fuel from the ruptured petrol tank pouring down on him.

This was a bad time to find out that there were no rescue crews on hand, no doctors or proper medical facilities on the circuit, and no removable steering wheel or any tools to get him out. He lay trapped in the car for twenty-five minutes, while fellow drivers struggled to free him, using tools borrowed from a spectator. Once out, he was dumped in the back of a pick-up truck, awaiting an ambulance. When the ambulance came, it was given a police escort to the hospital, but the escort managed to lose the ambulance and the driver did not know the way to the hospital.

This was all part of an amazingly lackadaisical approach to safety on the part of the governing body of the sport at that time. There were no full face helmets, no way of cutting off the electrics to prevent sparks in a crashed car and even seatbelts were not compulsory; the pits were not separated from the circuit by crash barriers and petrol stood around the pits in churns, just waiting to be crashed into. The circuits themselves were surrounded by trees and other solid objects, as Stewart had discovered to his cost.

The events of that afternoon understandably left a strong impression on Stewart. At future races he provided his own doctor and his team provided an ambulance for the benefit of any of the drivers who needed it. Stewart taped a spanner to his steering wheel, to make it more easily removable in an accident, and cut-out switches were introduced to make the electrics in a crashed car safe. Many of the other safety improvements to circuits and cars since then are down to his campaigning.

Hunt the Shunt

Jackie Stewart was a consummate professional; it was said that he would even forgo normal marital relations for a week before a race, so as not to interfere with his concentration. Nobody ever accused our other 1970s world champion of the like. For one thing, James Hunt could not have normal marital relations, since he had effectively 'sold' his wife Suzy to Richard Burton earlier in his world championship year. Mr and Mrs Hunt met the Burtons at a time when Burton's second marriage to Elizabeth Taylor was breaking down and Hunt was realising that he was not the marrying kind

(not that this stopped him repeatedly trying). Richard Burton and Suzy Hunt were attracted to each other and he and James Hunt did a deal whereby, if Hunt got divorced, Burton would underwrite a $1 million divorce settlement. The Burtons and the Hunts both got 'quickie' divorces on the same day (in Port au Prince, Haiti) and Richard Burton and Suzy Hunt married soon afterwards.

Hunt's preparation for the Japanese Grand Prix of 1976, at which he won his world championship, sums up his lifestyle. It was a two-week blur induced by alcohol, cannabis and cocaine, in the company of his friend Barry Sheene, the equally libertine motorcycle-racing champion. If Jackie Stewart was near-Olympic standard at shooting, Hunt was certainly Olympian, had his particular specialism been included in the games. In the two weeks before the Grand Prix, he claimed to have slept with no fewer than thirty-three British Airways stewardesses, part of a total of an alleged 5,000 conquests in a lifetime of excess.

In between all of this, he managed to fit in a motor-racing career. Hunt was born in 1947, the son of a London stockbroker. He was a rebellious and hyperactive child, intensely competitive. He attended his first motor-race meeting at the age of 18 and promptly decided that he was going to world champion. His parents unsurprisingly refused to bankroll this fanciful notion and he was forced to take on odd jobs to finance the preparation of a racing mini. Two years' work came to naught when the scrutineers refused to let him race, on the grounds (among other things) that his driver's seat was made from an old garden chair.

Eventually he got to compete and developed a reputation as a fast but accident-prone driver – something which gave him his nickname, 'Hunt the Shunt'. In time he came to the attention of Lord Alexander Hesketh, an eccentric aristocrat who was busily working his way through the family fortune in a hectic round of hedonistic pleasures. He had a motor-racing team and Hunt cut just the sort of glamorous playboy figure it needed. The pit lane was never dull when the Hesketh team were in town: the champagne flowed freely and they could scarcely move for pretty girls. Despite the ridicule of their more serious-minded opposition, the Hesketh team moved steadily through the formulas, finally entering the most glamorous and expensive – Formula 1 – in 1974. Those who thought team Hesketh were a joke were forced to reassess their opinions when Hunt beat Niki Lauda and his Ferrari to win the 1975 Dutch Grand Prix. But inevitably Lord Hesketh ran out of money at the end of the 1975 season and Hunt was left without a drive.

Luck intervened when Emerson Fittipaldi unexpectedly left McLaren, leaving them having to find a replacement driver at short notice. Hunt got the drive and by the last race of the 1976 season was running neck and neck with Niki Lauda for the championship. The start of the Japanese Grand Prix was hit by a violent rain storm. Conditions were so bad that, after a couple of laps, Niki Lauda retired his car, saying it was too dangerous to continue. Hunt stayed out in the deluge and drove fast enough to finish third, securing the world championship by a single point.

Hunt undoubtedly had charm, especially as far as the ladies were concerned, but he also displayed an overbearing conceit that twice had him voted the least-liked driver in Formula 1 by the motoring press. For all his swagger, though, he never overcame the attacks of nerves that led to him vomiting before a race and shaking violently as he prepared for the start. After his championship victory, motor racing gradually lost its charm for him as a driver and he retired in 1979, giving as his reason 'self-preservation'. He formed an unlikely but successful double act with the BBC's Murray Walker, commentating on motor racing. Typically, Hunt continued his bohemian ways in his new role, consuming two bottles of wine during the first Grand Prix on which he commentated, but his sometimes outspoken views gradually won the respect of his audience.

It is perhaps unsurprising that a life of excess finally caught up with him. On 15 June 1993 he proposed to what would have been his third wife, but on the same day suffered a massive and fatal heart attack. He was 45.

Football: The World Cup

England approached the 1970 World Cup in confident mood. As victors in 1966, they (and the hosts, Mexico) had automatic entry to the finals. They could still call upon several members of the 1966 squad and (in the eyes of most of the domestic press at least) they were favourites to retain it. The jingoistic coverage given them by the English media, coupled with their derogatory remarks about the host nation, ensured that they would get a pretty frosty reception from the locals and many non-aligned supporters.

One problem they faced was acclimatisation. The heat of Mexico was compounded by the fact that some of the venues were at altitude. In addition, the demands of worldwide television coverage meant that some of the matches had to kick off at midday, the very

hottest part of the day. Their preparation was also disturbed by their captain, Bobby Moore, being arrested in Colombia for allegedly stealing a bracelet from a jeweller's shop. He was only able to take part in the tournament after the authorities let him out on bail (the charge was subsequently quietly dropped).

The draw was not particularly kind to England, putting them in the same group as a Brazil side that came to be known as the greatest team ever to be fielded in a World Cup. It contained the great Pele, along with others – like Rivelino, Tostão and Gérson – who were scarcely less talented. England had the expected – though not overwhelming – victories over the other two members of the group, Romania and Czechoslovakia, but the match between England and Brazil turned out to be a classic. England put up a staunch defence against the brilliance of the Brazilians. Pele later described Bobby Moore as the greatest defender he had ever played against. Particularly memorable was an unbelievable feat of gymnastics produced by England goalkeeper Gordon Banks to keep out a Pele header, thought by many to have been the greatest save ever seen in a football match. England even had chances to win the game – Mullery hit the Brazilian bar and Astle somehow managed to miss an open goal from 10 yards. But in the end, not even Gordon Banks could do anything about the powerful shot from Jarzinho that settled the match in Brazil's favour.

But no matter: England went through to the knockout stages as runner-up in the group. In the quarter final we were drawn to meet our old rivals from the 1966 final, Germany. With twenty-two minutes to go, England were 2–0 up. Manager Alf Ramsey had made the decision to bring off Bobby Charlton, who until them had been a powerful presence in the midfield. Gordon Banks, the hero of the Brazil game, was out with food poisoning, and his stand-in, Peter Bonetti, let a German shot go under his body into the goal. Then, with just eight minutes to go, a header from Uwe Seller took the match into extra time, where the tournament's top scorer, Gerd Muller, scored the winner for Germany.

One unexpected loser from England's untimely exit from the tournament was (at least by his own reckoning) Harold Wilson. It was often claimed (rightly or wrongly) that the feel-good factor from England's 1966 World Cup triumph had helped to propel in a Labour government at that year's general election. (Fans of the arch-bigot Alf Garnett may recall his claim that England played the final in red shirts to make people think that Labour were responsible for the victory.) Harold Wilson had called the 1970 general election just four days after the match with Germany, and no doubt hoped to benefit again from some good vibrations from the result. In the event, the team lost and some of the politicians conducting last-minute election meetings following the match reported that the talk in the crowd was nothing to do with manifestos, and all to do with whether Peter Bonetti's goalkeeping errors or Alf Ramsey's substitutions were more responsible for the defeat. Just as England's football team were knocked out, so too was the Labour government.

What about 1974 and 1978? Err … I believe there were events calling themselves the World Cup held in 1974 and 1978, but since England failed to qualify for either they can hardly be regarded as

serious sporting occasions. However, I suppose we have to allow
our northern readers a moment's gloating, by admitting that
Scotland qualified for both of those finals. On both occasions they
were knocked out at the initial group stage, but the most humili-
ating of these came in 1978. Scotland qualified under their new
manager Ally McLeod, and he and the nation as a whole embarked
on (what seemed at least to Englishmen) an orgy of triumphalism.
Merchandisers went mad and their unofficial World Cup anthem
'Ally's Tartan Army' (which sold over 360,000 copies and made
number six in the charts) included the lines:

We're representing Britain, we're going to do or die
And England cannae do it, 'cos they did nae qualify

and

And we'll really shake them up
When we win the World Cup
'Cos Scotland is the greatest football team.

Scotland were reckoned to be in a relatively easy group. Apart
from having to face the previous cup's runners-up, Netherlands,
they had the mere formality of having to beat no-hopers Peru and
Iran to go through. In the event, they lost to Peru and could only
draw with Iran, leaving them needing an improbable three-goal
win against the Dutch. Premature celebration was replaced by
an outpouring of national grief. It was compounded by winger
Willie Johnson failing a drugs test and getting sent home, causing
the fans to change the lines of their song 'and we'll really shake
them up when we win the World Cup' to 'and we only take the
dope 'cos we haven't got a hope'. In the event, they got three
goals against the Netherlands, but unfortunately the opposition
also got two. Scotland were out and on their way home. Chrysler,
a major sponsor, withdrew its advertising; a record shop in

Dundee reduced the price of the 'Ally's Tartan Army' single from 65p to 1p, inviting customers to take some home to smash. The team were jeered at and spat upon when they landed at the airport. So that's quite enough gloating, thank you.

Horse Racing: Red Rum

One of the most celebrated sporting heroes of the 1970s had four legs, rather than two, and listed his sex as gelding. Red Rum was born in 1965, the foal of horses named Mared and Quorum (which explains his name, though conspiracy theorists will have noticed that it also spells 'murder' backwards). He was bred as a sprinter but earned his fame in one of the longest and most challenging of settings – the 4-mile 4-furlong Grand National course at Aintree.

It was touch and go whether he would have a racing career at all, since he suffered from pedal osteitis, an incurable bone disease of the feet. That he did succeed results from a chance taxi journey. Ginger McCain supplemented his earnings as a racehorse trainer with running a taxi and garage business. He got talking about racehorses with one of his fares and it transpired that the fare – a self-made millionaire named Noel Le Mare – was on the lookout for a horse that might be entered for the Grand National. He commissioned McCain to find one for him, McCain having a reputation for finding useful horses that others did not want. He found Red Rum, saw beyond the foot problem and bought him for his client for just 6,000 guineas.

As it happened, McCain was the ideal trainer for Red Rum. Having no gallops of his own, he used to exercise his horses on Southport Sands and it turned out that the sea water did Red Rum's foot condition a power of good. He was duly entered in the 1973 National, a relatively unfancied runner. Many people's favourite that year was a big Australian chaser called Crisp and, sure enough, Crisp made all of the running from start to finish, sometimes leading by as much as thirty lengths. By the last fence he was fifteen lengths ahead of Red Rum. But in the long run-in Red Rum steadily overhauled Crisp, catching him with about two strides to go and winning in a record time by three-quarters of a length, in what many think was the greatest Grand National finish of all time.

The following year Red Rum was made top weight for the National and the pundits were ready to write him off on account of the effect of the weight on his suspect feet. But Red Rum confounded them all with a second win. In the 1975 and 1976 races he could only manage second and by 1977 the critics were again trying to write him off, this time on account of his age. But Red Rum triumphed for an unprecedented third time, in what a poll of sports enthusiasts made the twenty-fourth greatest sporting moment of all time. He was due to be entered for the 1978 race, but the discovery of a hairline fracture the day before the race led to his withdrawal. Red Rum was a remarkable steeplechaser, as is illustrated by the fact that he never once fell in a hundred outings.

On his retirement, Red Rum entered a world of show business that made your average human celebrity look like a hermit. He opened supermarkets and leisure attractions, led the Grand National parade for many years, modelled for a wide range of Red Rum-related merchandise, turned on the Blackpool illuminations and made a guest appearance on the BBC's *Sports Personality of the Year* awards programme. When he died, in October 1995 at the age of 30, he was buried near the winning post at Aintree and the site has become a shrine for many racing enthusiasts. Eleven years after his death he was still Britain's best-known racehorse – indeed,

the best-known horse of any description. When a cross-section of the British public were asked to 'name an equine', 33 per cent came up with 'Black Beauty', but even he was comfortably beaten into second place by the 45 per cent who named Red Rum.

Olympic Glory

Munich – 1972: this was the second Olympics that the Germans had hosted. The first one, in 1936, had the unhappy association of having been run by Hitler as a Nazi propaganda event. To expunge that memory, the hosts decided that this competition would be known as the 'happy games'. For some, it was anything but.

The most memorable part of the games was the shooting. However, this took place not at the designated venue, but in the athletes' village. Eight Palestinian terrorists of the Black September organisation broke into the village and took a group of Israeli athletes and officials hostage. Two hostages were killed immediately and the rest subjected to an eighteen-hour stand-off with the authorities. Eventually the Germans made a botched rescue attempt, failing to send in enough rescuers, with the result that all of the hostages and five of the terrorists were killed. The three remaining offenders were imprisoned pending trial until the Germans felt obliged to exchange them for a hijacked Lufthansa jet. The Israeli secret police, Mossad, subsequently tracked down and executed two of them. The third is currently understood to be living 'somewhere in Africa', but is understandably coy about his precise whereabouts. These events, and the memorial service for the departed which followed, delayed the games by twenty-four hours.

The siege overshadowed the rest of the games. Mark Spitz, the American swimmer who had won a (then) record seven gold medals, was Jewish. It was feared that he would make too tempting a target for terrorists and he was forced to miss the closing ceremony. But it did not prevent the Cold War being extended into the sporting arena. The final of the men's basketball was between the

USA and Russia. Originally it was thought that America had won it 50–49 but, due to some misunderstanding on the part of the officials, the last three seconds of the match had to be rerun. During this, Russia scored, to win the match 51–50. The Americans protested furiously but in vain, eventually refusing to accept their silver medals.

The Americans suffered another disappointment in the men's 100 metres. Their two medal favourites, Rey Robinson and Eddie Hart, were rather too slow out of their starting blocks in their quarter finals. In fact, so slow were they that the others had finished long before they even got on track, as Robinson and Hart been told the wrong starting time for their events. Another American, marathon runner Frank Shorter, must have been confused as to whether he had won the gold or not. He was leading the event when a hoaxer joined the race for the final kilometre and entered the stadium in front of him. The crowd initially cheered what they thought must be the winner but, as officials ran to apprehend him, their cheers turned to boos. Shorter entered the stadium and was bewildered to see another athlete in front of him, being mysteriously assaulted, and the crowd booing vigorously when he had hoped for a bit of support for himself.

As for Britain, we entered one of the largest teams, of 284 athletes (210 of them men). The team included Britain's oldest ever Olympian, 69-year-old Lorna Johnstone. Fortunately she had a rather younger horse to help her get round the equestrian course. We competed in 159 events in eighteen sports, but the medal tally was rather modest – nine bronze, five silver and four gold – the latter being Mary Peters in the pentathalon, Richard Meade in the equestrian three-day event (where we also won the team gold) and Chris Davies and Rodney Pattison in a yachting event.

Montreal – 1976: in 1976, the problem was not so much unwelcome, uninvited visitors as those invitees who did not take part. The International Olympic Committee (IOC) had a choice of Montreal, Moscow and Los Angeles to host the 1976 games and one of the factors that led them to favour Montreal over the others was the fear of one superpower boycotting the other, in an extension of the Cold War. They need not have worried. Both the USA and Russia turned up. The problem was that most of Africa did not. The New Zealand rugby team had recently toured apartheid South Africa, outraging public opinion in many parts of the world. There were calls for the IOC to bar New Zealand in retaliation and when they declined to do so, twenty-six African nations withdrew from the games in protest. For good measure, the Republic of China (what we might know as Taiwan) withdrew after their Canadian hosts said they could not be allowed to compete under that name, on the grounds that Canada recognised the People's Republic of China. (As a footnote, the IOC did indeed experience the Cold War boycotts they had feared, when they awarded the next two games to Moscow and Los Angeles in 1980 and 1984.)

There was further controversy when Canadian Prime Minister Pierre Trudeau invited Queen Elizabeth, as the crowned head of Canada, to open the games. This stirred up republican feeling in Canada and there were calls for her to be uninvited, but it was too late. In any event, she could have been attending as a proud mother, since her daughter, Princess Anne, was a member of the British equestrian team (and the only female competitor not to be subjected to the indignity of a sex test). One place where such tests might have been useful was in the East German ladies' swimming team, whose unusually large muscles and deep voices led one of their American opponents to claim they had been on the steroids. An East German official replied, 'We have come here to swim, not to sing.' Generally the games were marked by many accusations of drug misuse, though relatively few were actually proved.

Definite cheating was unearthed in the Russian men's pentathalon team, where one Boris Onishchenko was found to have rigged his epee to sound a hit when none had been scored. As a result the entire Russian pentathalon team was disqualified, sending them rampaging through the team hotel with the intention of throwing Boris out of the window if they could find him.

One of the stars to emerge from the game was the Romanian gymnast Nadia Comăneci, who achieved seven perfect scores for one of her routines, bewildering the electronic scoreboard, which could not cope with a score that high. Another gymnast, Shun Fugimoto, helped his team to take the gold medal despite having broken his knee earlier in the competition.

The games were affected by rain, with a downpour putting out the Olympic flame. An unthinking official relit it with a cigarette lighter, causing his shocked colleagues to turn it off again and relight it with a spare piece of the real Olympic flame that they had kept in reserve for just such an eventuality.

Britain sent 249 representatives to the games and they came back with three gold, five silver and five bronze medals. Our golden boys (there were no golden girls) were the men's pentathalon team, John Osborn and Reginald White in the sailing and David Wilkie in the men's 200 metres breast stroke. The nearest we got to glory in athletics was Brendan Foster's bronze in the 10,000 metres.

One definite loser from the games was Canada. It cost the country a mind-boggling $1.6 billion (Canadian) to stage them and left the government with a debt that took thirty years to pay off. The main stadium, originally referred to as 'the big O', came to be known locally as 'the big owe'.

Not So Lovely Cricket: Basil D'Oliveira and Kerry Packer

As I write this, England is smarting under the humiliation of a whitewash test defeat against Australia. It is therefore comforting to look back to the test match series of the 1970s. In four of the six series England were left holding the Ashes and in two of these series (1970–71 and 1977) the Australians failed to win a single test match. But much of the most interesting cricketing action of the 1970s took place off the field.

The break-up of cricket's established order started with the Basil D'Oliveira affair in the late 1960s. D'Oliveira was a South African-born all-rounder, but under apartheid he was racially classified as 'coloured', which meant that he could not play first-class cricket in his home country. He emigrated to England, where he qualified to play for the national team, and did so in forty-four test matches. Come the 1968–69 tour to South Africa, the English selectors were faced with a tricky problem, for a side containing D'Oliveira would clearly be unacceptable to their hosts.

Initially, the selectors left D'Oliveira out of the side, supposedly for purely cricketing reasons, though whether the real reason was moral cowardice remains a matter for debate to this day. But when one of the squad, Tom Cartwright, dropped out, they decided to make the controversial selection. Meanwhile the South African government had been doing its best to engineer the outcome, by trying to bribe D'Oliveira to declare himself unavailable and making all sorts of dark threats to the MCC and the test selectors. When the selection was finally made, South Africa said a side

containing D'Oliveira would not be welcome and England called
the tour off. Shortly afterwards, in 1971, the Commonwealth
countries enshrined their opposition to racism in the Singapore
Declaration (and later the 1979 Gleneagles Agreement) which
isolated South Africa as a cricketing nation until the dismantling of
apartheid. Meanwhile, many of the top South African players took
part in a series of unofficial England *v.* the Rest of the World tests,
though these were not recognised by cricket's world governing
body, the International Cricket Council.

A more fundamental shake-up of cricket was to follow in the
mid-1970s, in the form of Kerry Packer. Packer was an immensely
wealthy Australian media tycoon who was also a sports enthusiast. He saw increased sporting coverage as an essential part of
the development of his television interests, but was frustrated
by the unwillingness of the Australian Cricket Board (ACB) to
countenance him covering their sport. The board had a long-term
relationship with the broadcaster ABC (Australia's equivalent to
our BBC) despite Packer being willing to offer eight times more
than his rival for the broadcasting rights. Packer characterised

this as an old pals' network, especially when ABC had its contract renewed for a fraction of Packer's offer.

Packer's abrasive negotiating style may have had something to do with his lack of success with the cricket board. When they met in 1976, his opening pitch to them apparently was: 'There is a little bit of the whore in all of us, gentlemen. What is your price?' One breakthrough he did have was with England's Test and County Cricket Board (TCCB), after the ACB tried to get the TCCB to sell their test coverage rights to their pals in ABC for just 14 per cent of what Packer was offering. Packer promptly doubled his offer and secured the rights.

Faced with this domestic brick wall, Packer began secretly assembling an assortment of the world's best players to take part in something called World Series Cricket (WSC). He was helped by the fact that the national cricket bodies then paid their international players peanuts for representing their countries. One of his chief recruiters was the then England captain Tony Greig, and among his signings were the captains of the West Indies, Australia (both past and current) and India (future). But initially they had no grounds on which to play and no administration to back it up.

When word of this accidentally got out to the media in May 1977, the cricketing establishment went ballistic. Greig was stripped of his England captaincy and ostracised at home, and around the world attempts were made to exclude WSC signatories from the game. Perhaps unsurprisingly, Packer's attempts to negotiate a settlement came to naught and it all ended up in the high court, with Packer accusing the cricketing authorities of restraint of trade. Characteristically, Packer hired the country's top ten QCs for the duration of the trial, not necessarily with a view to using their services, but with instructions to them not to accept any additional work (i.e. for the other side) during the trial. The case went Packer's way, with the cricket authorities having to pay costs.

WSC got off to a slow start, with very poor attendances, but the coverage of the game brought about many innovations – coloured strip, day–night and more one-day matches (and better pay for the players). Packer made extensive use of aggressive fast bowlers, seeing them as being more televisual than spinners, but, after a player got his jaw broken by a bouncer, cricket helmets were introduced by WSC. (The jaw-breaking incident did their ratings no harm at all!) Meanwhile the official Australian team – particularly hard-hit by WSC defections – performed very badly in their test series.

By the second season, attendances for the World Series were at near capacity but both the ACB and Packer were by now starting to feel the financial strain. A deal was struck, much to the annoyance of some of the other national cricket bodies, which felt betrayed. WSC was eventually wound up, but Packer got his television rights and the face of cricket was changed forever.

Lovely Boating Weather

The only possible interest the University Boat Race can have for a real sporting enthusiast is if one of the boats sinks. The 1970s had nothing to compare with the classic years of the event, like 1912 when both crews sank, or 1984, when Cambridge spared us the necessity of watching the race by obligingly crashing into a moored barge and sinking during the warm-up. But at least there was 1978. Cambridge had been soundly thrashed by Oxford the previous year, but had high hopes of reversing their fortunes in 1978. They were in second place (or as we would call it, last) but not yet sufficiently last to plunge them into despair, as they rounded the Surrey bend. At that point they encountered a strong wind, which was whipping up waves more suited to surfers than oarsmen. For some reason, the Cambridge boat (unlike its rival) had taken to the water without fitting any splashboards, something which a member of the crew later described as 'an act of monumental idiocy'. Few would have argued with his assessment as boat and crew disappeared majestically beneath the waves.

9

Two Prime Ministers

Two new leaders of the main political parties were elected at about the same time in the mid-1970s and, on the face of it, they could not have been more different. Both served as prime minister, and we will follow their separate careers – but only as far as the end of our decade.

Sunny Jim

Jim Callaghan was born in Portsmouth in 1912, the son of an Irish naval petty officer. He passed the Senior Oxford Certificate but his father had died when he was 9 and his mother could not afford to send him to university. Instead he went to work as a clerk in the Inland Revenue. While there, he played a leading part in setting up their trade union, the Association of Officers of Taxes, and in 1931 he became a member of the Labour Party. By 1936 he was a full-time official with what was by then known as the Inland Revenue Staff Federation.

His work with the union brought him into contact with the socialist academic Harold Laski, who encouraged him both to stand for Parliament and to study and lecture at the London School of Economics. But the war intervened and he joined the navy as an ordinary seaman. He rose to the rank of lieutenant by 1944, at which time he was diagnosed with tuberculosis and discharged. During the latter stages of the war he was made Labour parliamentary candidate for Cardiff South, and was duly elected in the Labour landslide of 1945. He would go on to represent parliamentary seats in Cardiff until 1987. By 1947 he was parliamentary secretary to the Ministry of Transport, where he was responsible (among other things) for the introduction of zebra crossings.

Popular with his colleagues, Callaghan was elected to the Shadow Cabinet every year from 1951 to 1964, and ran (unsuccessfully) for deputy leader of the party in 1960 and leader in 1963. In the latter election he came third behind Harold Wilson and George Brown, but attracted a good deal of support from the right wing of the party, who did not trust either of the leading candidates.

In 1964, Labour was elected into power and Callaghan was made Chancellor of the Exchequer. He inherited the post at a time of financial crisis, with a balance of payments deficit, speculators attacking sterling, high inflation and high unemployment. His solution involved substantial tax increases, which did not go down well with the public. Despite that, Labour won a further general election in 1966. More destabilising chaos followed, with

a Middle East crisis, oil price rises and an eight-week national dock strike, among other woes. In November 1967 the pound was devalued by 14.3 per cent and Callaghan felt honour-bound to tender his resignation. Harold Wilson refused to accept it and instead arranged a job swap between Callaghan and Roy Jenkins, the Home Secretary.

This was out of the international-exchange-rates frying pan and into the fire that was the Northern Ireland troubles. It was Callaghan who took the decision to send the troops into the province. He also brought in the Commonwealth Immigrants Act 1968, limiting Commonwealth immigration to the United Kingdom, and the Race Relations Act, making it illegal to discriminate on the grounds of race. On the trade union front, he led the opposition to Barbara Castle's *In Place of Strife* (discussed elsewhere in the book) and instead played a leading role in developing the ill-fated social contract with the unions.

Following the 1974 election victory, Callaghan was appointed Foreign Secretary and was responsible for successfully renegotiating the terms of Britain's membership of the Common Market. When Harold Wilson stepped down as prime minister in 1976, he unofficially endorsed Callaghan to succeed him, despite his age (he was 64, and would be the oldest person to become prime minister since Winston Churchill). Callaghan was duly appointed on 5 April 1976, and still remains the only politician to have held all the four great offices of state. His premiership was dogged by being a minority government in the Commons, along with all the other British malaises of the period – double-digit inflation, trade union militancy and high unemployment. It all culminated in the Winter of Discontent and electoral defeat in May 1979.

Callaghan stayed on as Labour leader until October 1980, and as a Member of Parliament until 1987, thereafter becoming Baron Callaghan of Cardiff. He died in 2005, the day before his ninety-third birthday.

The things he said:

On leadership:
'A leader has to appear consistent. That doesn't mean he has to be consistent.'
'A leader must have the courage to act against an expert's advice.'

On the state of 1970s Britain:
'If I were a young man I would emigrate.'

On Margaret Thatcher over devolution:
'We can truly say that once the Leader of the Opposition had discovered what the Liberals and the Scottish National Party were going to do, she found the courage of their convictions.'

On his treatment of Barbara Castle and colleagues over In Place of Strife:
'I wasn't stabbing them in the back, I was stabbing them in the front.'

On the social contract:
'What Britain needs is a new social contract' (a statement made on 2 October 1972).
'I say to both sides of industry please don't support us with general expressions of goodwill and kind words, and then undermine us through unjustified wage increases or price increases. Either back us or sack us.'

What others said about him:

'Jim Callaghan was a formidable opponent, one who could best me across the despatch box. In other circumstances he would have been a successful prime minister. He was a superb party manager. Despite our disagreements I always respected him because I knew he was moved by deep patriotism.' – Margaret Thatcher (in an obituary to Callaghan)

'Jim is a much better prime minister than Wilson. He is much more candid and open with people and doesn't try to double-talk them as Wilson did.' – Tony Benn

'There is nobody in politics that I can remember and no case I can think of in history where a man combined such a powerful political personality with so little intelligence.' – Roy Jenkins

'The Keeper of the Cloth Cap.' – Journalist Peter Jenkins

'The champion of moderation, common sense and national unity.' – *The Times*

Attila the Hen

The 1970s saw the rise to prominence of Britain's longest-serving prime minister of the twentieth century, and one of the most influential – and controversial – British politicians of the period. Most of the facts of her background are too well known to require repetition in any detail.

Margaret Roberts was born in 1925, the daughter of a prosperous grocer from Grantham in Lincolnshire, a town described by one of its former town clerks as 'a narrow town, built on a narrow street and inhabited by narrow people'. The family were Methodists (or, to be precise, Wesleyan – a nicer class of Methodist). She later transferred to the Church of England – the Conservative party at prayer – though she never abandoned the Wesleyan principles of hard work, public service and self-improvement and the condemnation of frivolity and idleness. Her father was for twenty-five years a pillar of the council (and its one-time mayor), and a leading light in the Rotary Club and the Trustee Savings Bank. He paid for Margaret to have private tuition for Oxford University and funded her degree in chemistry.

At Oxford she became president of the university Conservative Association and, after graduating, married the wealthy Burmah Oil director Dennis Thatcher in 1951. She had two unsuccessful runs for Parliament at Dartford, in the 1950 and 1951 elections, in which the local area agent praised her as 'an amazing young woman with quite outstanding ability'. She finally secured the safe seat of Finchley in 1959, and by 1961 was a parliamentary under-secretary in the Ministry of Pensions and National Insurance in Harold Macmillan's administration.

When Edward Heath became leader of the opposition in 1966, he was advised that he needed a token woman in his Cabinet (the previous token woman, Mervyn Pike, having retired) and that Mrs Thatcher was the best of the available bunch. Heath was initially not keen (and became increasingly less so, as familiarity lent disenchantment to the relationship). Woodrow Wyatt, writing in the *Sunday Mirror* in December 1969, shared Heath's doubts: 'her air of bossiness, her aptitude for interfering, can be very tiring and irritating to easy-going men who do not always want to be kept up to scratch, particularly by a female', and fellow Cabinet members variously described her as 'governessy', a corporal rather than a cavalry officer and a jumped-up housemaid.

Regardless of what they thought, in June 1970 she was made Education Secretary, where she is mostly (and wrongly) remem-bered for stopping school milk for the over-7s in primary schools. The reality was that Labour had already stopped it in secondary schools, and that this cut was imposed by the Treasury, against her wishes. She was nonetheless demonised for it, as 'Thatcher the milk snatcher'. Her real achievements in the post included saving the Open University from cuts, raising the school leaving age to 16, introducing a new nursery school programme and closing more grammar schools (over 3,200) than any other Education Secretary before or since.

After Heath lost two elections in less than a year in 1974, his position as leader of the Conservatives looked increasingly unten-able. The influential back-bench 1922 Committee, which was not short of Heath's enemies among its membership, decided within four days of the second 1974 election defeat that there should be a party leadership contest. Thatcher had expected to support the candidacy of her friend Keith Joseph. But he ruled himself out, not least with an extraordinarily ill-judged speech in Birmingham, in which he advocated birth control for the lower orders to prevent them producing a new generation of delinquent problem children. Edward Du Cann, another possible candidate, was prevented from standing by his questionable reputation in the city and Reginald Maudling (already twice a candidate for the Conservative leadership) had been ruled out by his involvement in the Poulson scandal.

In the absence of any candidate who reflected her views Thatcher decided to stand herself. Her campaign manager was Airey Neave MP, who was himself on a mission to oust Heath after falling out with him. Heath ran an incompetent campaign, partly over-confident, partly over-ingratiating, while Thatcher, helped by Neave's ability as a deal-maker, quietly made ground. Neave deliberately underplayed the progress she was making, content to let people think she was merely the stalking horse for a more favoured candidate. In the event, she surprised everyone (except possibly herself) by beating Heath by 130–119 in the first ballot. Heath immediately resigned and a second ballot was held in which several Tory grandees put themselves forward. This time Willy Whitelaw was favourite to win.

In February 1975, to the mingled amazement and even horror of some in the party, she was elected Conservative leader, beating Whitelaw by seventy-seven votes. (The reaction of a Conservative vice president to news of her victory was 'My God! The bitch has won!') It was said that she was elected because her ministerial track record had shown her to be a pragmatist, rather than an ideologue. Heath was never reconciled to being usurped and henceforth, partly through his behaviour towards her, became known as the 'Incredible Sulk'.

At first the media, fascinated by the idea of a female party leader, were more interested in her housework regime and fashion choices than her political creed. But she soon managed to get across the message that she was the champion of what she called middle-class values – encouraging choice, preventing the state from becoming too powerful and promoting private property as a bulwark of individual freedom.

She had a shaky start, in which her approval rating almost halved to 35 per cent in her first four months as leader. Many in her own party predicted that she would be out by Christmas. Increasingly involved with the right-wing Institute of Economic Affairs, which opposed such orthodoxies as the welfare state and Keynesian economics, she developed a platform built on less government, lower taxes and more individual freedoms. She also started to make a mark in international politics (if not necessarily international diplomacy). A January 1976 speech in which she strongly attacked the Soviet Union earned her the Russian soubriquet the 'Iron Lady' – a title she relished.

By 1978, as the Labour government neared the end of its term of office, the economic outlook was looking rather better than in 1974 and forecasters began to talk in terms of a further Labour general election win. But, as we have seen elsewhere, Prime Minister James Callaghan made a fatal mistake in not going to the country in the autumn of 1978. What followed became known as the Winter of Discontent, with masses of highly visible strikes and rising unemployment that enabled the Conservatives to coin the election slogan, 'Labour isn't working'. By May 1979 public opinion had swung away from them again. The Conservatives were elected with a forty-four-seat majority, Britain had its first female prime minister and the rest – as they say – is history.

But even as she approached her moment of triumph, Margaret Thatcher was not a universal hit with the electorate. A 1978 poll suggested that the Conservatives' narrow 3 per cent lead would have risen to 14 per cent if Heath had replaced her. Given the mess of the Winter of Discontent, over which her opponents had presided, one might have thought a Conservative victory was

a foregone conclusion, but she lagged consistently behind the incumbent prime minister, James Callaghan, in personal popularity. At the start of the campaign she was 7 per cent behind; by the start of May this had reached 19 per cent. Even four out of ten Conservative voters thought Callaghan would be a better prime minister than her. She was seen as less experienced, less in touch with ordinary people, as well as being strident and condescending. One newspaper said she was like an angry woodpecker at the despatch box. Not all who eventually learned to love her had yet done so.

The things she said:

About the sexes:
'Power is like being a lady … If you have to tell people you are, you aren't.'
'If you want something said, ask a man. If you want something done, ask a woman.'
'I usually make up my mind about a man in ten seconds, and I very rarely change it.'

About socialism:
'The trouble with socialism is that you eventually run out of other people's money.'

About compromise:
'To me, consensus seems to be the process of abandoning all beliefs, principles, values and policies. So it is something in which no one believes and to which no one objects.'
'If you set out to be liked, you would be prepared to compromise on anything at any time, and you would achieve nothing.'
'One of the great problems of our age is that we are governed by people who care more about feelings than they do about thoughts and ideas.'
'I don't mind how much the ministers talk, as long as they do what I say.'

About criticism:
'If my critics saw me walking over the Thames they would say it was because I couldn't swim.'

About self-confidence:
'As God once said, and I think rightly …'

About the Falklands:

American diplomat Alexander Haig questioned why she was going to war over islands that were thousands of miles away, had a handful of citizens, and were politically and economically insignificant. 'Just like Hawaii, I imagine,' Thatcher replied.

The things other people said about her:

'Attila the Hen' – Clement Freud MP

'A bargain basement Boadicea' – Denis Healey MP

'The thought that she might not be right has never crossed Mrs Thatcher's mind. It is a strength in a politician' – Roy Hattersley MP

'Methodism, science and suburbia had armoured her in self-confidence and self-righteousness' – journalist Simon Jenkins

'She is in love: in love with power, success and with herself' – Barbara Castle MP (who appears to have meant this as a compliment)

'Reality hasn't really intervened in my mother's life since the 1970s' – daughter Carol Thatcher

'Like a cat sliding down a blackboard' – Clive James' description of her voice in 1973 (She later worked with a voice coach to soften her delivery and iron out her Lincolnshire accent.)

'The party would never put up with those hats or that accent' – Enoch Powell, prior to 1979, on her party leadership prospects

10

British Leyland

The decline and fall of the British car industry is a story that extends considerably – and painfully – on either side of our chosen decade, but its death throes were particularly pronounced during the 1970s. The independent British car industry (that is, those manufacturers that were not sub-divisions of American giants like Ford or General Motors) had been in trouble since the war, with too many manufacturers to enjoy economies of scale, too many models, often competing fruitlessly with each other, and a range of models which were either fit for retirement to the National Motor Museum, or newer, but hopelessly under-developed and/or unprofitable.

In 1968 the British car industry (encouraged by Tony Benn and the Labour government's Industrial Reorganisation Committee) decided to consolidate all its little problems into one huge headache, which it called British Leyland (BL). It involved the merger of the failing British Motor Holdings (BMH), Britain's largest car manufacturer, selling marques like Austin, Morris and MG, with the relatively more successful Leyland Motor Corporation (LMC), producer of Triumph and Rover, among others, as well as a lot of commercial vehicles. It created the world's fourth largest car maker, with 40 per cent of the domestic car market, at the time of the merger. It was hoped that Leyland's business expertise could be used to pull BMH out of the mire and LMC's chairman, Sir Donald Stokes, was given the poisoned chalice of running the new conglomerate. Instead, the problems of BMH and the unwieldy nature of the merged company dragged the lot of them down. By 1980 that 40 per cent share of the home market would shrink to 18.2 per cent.

Stokes inherited a real ragbag of a company, with eighteen brands making up British Leyland. These were being built in around forty manufacturing facilities. Now these competing companies became part of the same organisation. This had been creating problems for years – for as long as the growing company and its predecessors had been absorbing other players in the British car industry. Back in the 1950s, when MG had wanted to produce its first real post-war sports car, the MGA, it was stopped from doing so for a number of years because it would have competed with the Austin Healey that the company was about to launch. Now, internal competition was endemic. At the time of the takeover, the competing models that were being produced within the company included:

Morris Minor and Austin 1100
Austin 1300 and Triumph Herald
Morris Marina and Triumph Dolomite
Triumph 2000, Rover 2000 and Austin Princess
Triumph Spitfire, MG Midget and Austin-Healey Sprite
Triumph TR6 and TR7 and the MGB
Rover 3500 and Jaguar XJ6

To be fair, one of the company's first efforts to rationalise this confusion was a success. The Rover P6 and the Triumph 2000 were after the same customers, but both were superseded by the Rover SD1, which won European Car of the Year.

Duplication between the different areas of the new organisation also extended to parts. British Leyland found that it was producing two different 1.3-litre engines, two 1.5s, two V8s and no fewer than four different 2-litre engines.

BMH were also past masters at badge engineering (that is, selling identical or near-identical models under different makers' names, so that, for example, the early Minis could be had as the Austin 7, the Morris Mini-Minor, the Riley Elf or the Wolseley Hornet). It did little or nothing for overall sales and diluted the effect of the marketing effort (which was itself confused enough by attempts to establish British Leyland as a brand in its own right). Their marketing was more generally misguided; they largely ignored the potential of European markets (and the threat that continental manufacturers posed to domestic sales) and concentrated on less profitable Commonwealth markets. In 1950, Britain had made 52 per cent of the entire world's car exports (partly because most American production went to the domestic market and the French and German industries had not yet recovered from the effects of the war). By 1974 we were only the sixth largest car exporter, and our penetration of the vital French, German and Italian markets was negligible (1.3 per cent, 0.6 per cent and 0.4 per cent respectively).

The multitude of British Leyland makes and models meant there was never enough volume in any one model's sales to pay for the cost of properly developing its successor. So models would stagger on long after they should have been updated (for example, Stokes found when he took over BMH in 1968 that there were no plans afoot to replace the Morris Minor (introduced in 1948) or the Austin Cambridge (from 1959)). When new models were finally introduced, either the urgency of their introduction and/ or a lack of resources meant that their development was rushed and/or under-financed. Even that cultural icon the early Mini had problems, including a dodgy gear-change, engine electrics that could not cope with heavy rain and a severely leaky passenger compartment (motoring journalists recommended keeping goldfish in the door pockets). To make matters worse, the Mini, though it sold in huge numbers, never made much money for the manufacturer, owing to the company's suicidal pricing policy, designed to undercut competition from the likes of Ford.

Moreover, there was a 'make do and mend' approach to product development. The looks of the Austin Maxi were not improved by having to use the doors from the larger Austin 1800 model, the Morris Marina was a Frankenstein's monster, cobbled together out of various bits of other BL models (including the 1948 Morris Minor), and the Allegro would have been less dumpy-looking, had the designer not been forced by the men in suits to enlarge the bonnet to accommodate an outdated 'tall' engine.

The inherent design faults in many of the models were compounded by shortcomings in their build quality. BL could not get it right even for prestige clients. It secured the rights to provide the cars for the popular television series *The Professionals*, a piece of product placement for which most manufacturers would have given their eye teeth. But its cars proved so unreliable that they caused delays in the filming schedules and a frustrated television company eventually switched to Fords. The Board of Trade sent back the small fleet of Princesses it had ordered since there were so many faults with them. Not even the prime minister was immune. In 1978, Downing Street ordered two prime minis- terial Rovers, with armour plating and bullet-proof windows. When first delivered, the cars were found to have thirty-four mechanical faults, and they were sent back. On their return,

Prime Minister Callaghan went out for a spin in one. He pressed the button to open his electronic bullet-proof window and the window promptly fell into his lap. He did not use the car again.

To the challenge of trying to market this unappetising range of models must be added a perfect storm of adverse circumstances, including labour relations that were a legend for awfulness (of which more later), incompetent management, the 1973 oil crisis, the three-day week and galloping inflation. By 1975, the company was heading merrily towards bankruptcy. A report on the state of BL by Sir Don Ryder was presented to the government. His report aimed to tell the government what it wanted to hear, for it laid the blame for BL's plight mainly at the door of world economic conditions, rather than any shortcomings of the company itself. Moreover, his wildly over-ambitious forecasts of BL's future (which had the company maintaining domestic market share and increasing European sales by 25 per cent within seven years) encouraged the government into becoming a major shareholder. The company was reorganised into four divisions:

Leyland Cars: still the UK's largest car manufacturer, with about 128,000 employees in thirty-six locations and a potential capacity of a million vehicles a year;

Leyland Truck and Bus: the UK's largest commercial and passenger vehicle maker, producing 38,000 trucks, 19,000 tractors and 8,000 buses a year;

Two specialist divisions, dealing with a wide range of specialist products, and with exports and overseas manufacturing.

One person who was not convinced by Ryder was the new Conservative leader, Margaret Thatcher. Her conclusion was that 'Unless we can ensure a flourishing and competitive industry capable of producing a product at a price people will pay, it is not only the future of British Leyland that is at stake, but the very standards and standing of the British nation itself.'

But even Mrs Thatcher, once prime minister, put public money into BL – after all, there were a lot of marginal seats in car-making constituencies. BL would get through the modern equivalent of £11 billion of taxpayers' money before it finally went under. There was even a suggestion that the overseas aid budget should be raided to buy unwanted BL trucks, which could then be given, in lieu of aid, to impoverished third world nations.

In 1977 a South African businessman, Sir Michael Edwardes, became the company's chief executive. He drew up a plan of rationalisation that would virtually halve the workforce within five years, closing nineteen plants. Leyland Cars was again sub-divided, this time into Austin-Morris (the high-volume part of the market) and Jaguar Rover Triumph (upmarket and specialist vehicles). In 1979 the name British Leyland Ltd was shortened to BL Ltd.

By the end of the 1970s, the threat from overseas competition became depressingly clear. In 1955, just 2.2 per cent of the cars bought by British motorists were foreign. In 1975 the figure was up to 33 per cent and by 1980 almost 57 per cent. German car makers were exporting ten times as many cars as the British industry that had once been world market leader.

Most of the Leyland plants are now gone and most of the surviving brands are in foreign hands. Jaguar and Land Rover are now part of India's Tata motors. What is left of Rover and MG (which is not a lot) now rests with China's Nanjing Automobile. Parts of the commercial vehicle business went to DAF in the Netherlands and to Sweden's Volvo, and the Cowley plant for building the new Mini is owned by Germany's BMW. In 1986 Britain saw the first of the Japanese manufacturers arrive, when Nissan opened its Sunderland plant. Today, Nissan is Britain's largest car manufacturer.

Labour Relations and 'Red Robbo'

In the 1970s, labour relations in the car industry – and in British Leyland in particular – were a by-word for what was wrong with British industry generally. They also gave the tabloid media

a headline-making demon into which to stick their editorial pins – Derek Robinson, or 'Red Robbo'. Robinson (1927–) was indeed a committed life-long communist. He stood as their candidate in four general elections, losing his deposit every time and only once polling more than 1 per cent of the vote; he would later become national chair of the Communist Party of Great Britain during the 1990s. He was apprenticed into the car industry during the Second World War, where he naturally became an active trade unionist. He rose through the ranks until, by 1975, he had succeeded another communist, Dick Etheridge, as union convenor of BL's Longbridge plant in Birmingham. In the years that followed, Robinson and his network of union organisers in forty-two BL plants staged a long series of strikes in different parts of BL, in protest, he said, against the company's mismanagement.

Certainly mismanagement was not in short supply within the organisation. When Sir Michael Edwardes took over, he was amazed to find that nobody could even tell him which parts of the organisation were profitable and which loss-making, and when the new Triumph TR7 was launched with a host of faults, the men on the production line (who could see how to remedy some of them) found that there was no means for a factory of 2,500 men to communicate their ideas to the management. There was a classic dispute in 1979, lasting several weeks, when workers went on strike after losing out on a pay rise by missing productivity targets. It turned out that nobody had thought to tell them what those targets were. However, in fairness, not every part of BL management was incompetent. George Turnbull and a number of his colleagues were head-hunted by the South Koreans and set up their very successful Hyundai car company.

The way in which British Leyland had developed, absorbing other manufacturers incrementally and inheriting their separate production facilities, was another factor in BL's labour relations problems. The Ryder report showed that there were 246 separate pay-bargaining units within BL. The car division alone had fifty-eight bargaining units and 324 separate pay rates. The main-tenance (or erosion) of pay differentials thus became an ongoing nightmare for all concerned. Demarcation was another fruitful source of industrial unrest; in September 1975, 21,000 workers walked out over a dispute about who pushed the buttons on a new control panel.

Worse, localised disputes could result in entire plants being shut down. In late 1975, 16,000 BL workers found themselves laid off as a result of a localised dispute in one small component supplier. In another dispute at Leyland's Triumph plant in Speke, twenty-one men in the trim workshop complained about a smell made by stray cats. Work was stopped and cleaners brought in. After forty-five minutes scrubbing, the workers were invited to return to their jobs, but they complained that the floor was still wet, creating dangerous work conditions. Two days later, the floor had apparently still not dried to their satisfaction and 600 other workers in the plant had been sent home.

It is perhaps not surprising that the productivity of the British car worker lagged far behind its overseas competition. In the late 1970s, the average British car worker produced five cars a year, compared with twelve for a Japanese worker and fifteen for an American. Whilst part of this was undoubtedly down to over-manning (for which management and unions can share the blame) it was also due to the fact that most of the plants were thoroughly outdated. Only with the introduction of the Mini Metro did the company start to get to grips with the automation revolution that was taking place elsewhere in car-making technology. This may have reflected the company's unwillingness to invest. Over seven years, BL made a net profit of £74 million, of which £70 million went straight into the shareholders' pockets.

Demonised though he was by the media, Robinson was not necessarily the most militant of the British Leyland workers. He spent a lot of time trying (not always with conspicuous success) to prevent unofficial strikes. In the first six months of 1977, strikes lost the company 9.3 million man hours and 120,000 cars. Robinson also wanted to develop the idea of 'participation', with union officials and the firm's management working together to make the company a success. Naturally, there was also a political dimension to the idea. He said, 'If we make Leyland successful, it will be a political victory. It will prove that ordinary working people have got the intelligence and determination to run industry.' It is even claimed in some quarters that the pursuit of this idea led to a breakdown in the relationship between union officials (now seen as 'the bosses' men') and the shop floor, which damaged the unions' ability to control unofficial strikes. A further complication was that the union was ideologically split, with the Cowley plant (where the union officials tended to be Trotskyites, rather than communists) tending to be more militant than Longbridge.

Militant or not, BL management and the incoming Conservative government in 1979 were keen to see the back of Red Robbo. In the late 1970s, MI5 tried to undermine him by planting one of their agents among his union officials. In November 1979 they got their chance. He put his name to a pamphlet, criticising BL management, and refused to withdraw it when asked to do so. He was sacked and inevitably the workers were asked to come out in sympathy. For once, they rejected the strike call, by a margin of 14,000 to 600. According to the BBC, 'between 1978 and 1979 Mr Robinson was credited with causing 523 walkouts at Longbridge, costing an estimated £200 million in lost production'.

11

Conspiracy!

A Climate of Fear

'Tanks on the streets. The prime minister toppled. The Cabinet imprisoned on the *QE2*. Fiction? No. Thirty years ago a secret cabal of generals, aristocrats and businessmen really did plot to oust Harold Wilson and seize power.' (*Daily Mail*, 2006, as quoted in *The State – a warning to the Labour movement*, a pamphlet first produced by 'Militant' and reissued on the Internet in 2006).

Britain's instability in the 1970s lent weight (for those who were so inclined) to the view that Britain was in imminent danger of falling apart. It was not just isolated wild-eyed fanatics who harboured these fears; Lord Robens, former chairman of the National Coal Board, expressed fears on television that Britain was heading towards a dictatorship of the right or left – he was not sure which – and a senior statesman of the Conservative Party, Lord Hailsham, told journalist Hugo Young that democracy could not survive the rate of inflation the nation was currently running. He went on:

> People will not put up with the law being broken and factions of the workers getting away with it with impunity. People will take control into their own hands, or a strong government will

use the public forces to take control. People will get hurt. Quite
likely there will be a lot of violence one way or another. But in
the end there is a limit to what middle-class people will tolerate.

Nor was it just right-wing paranoia. Labour Foreign Secretary Jim
Callaghan told a 1974 ministerial seminar, 'If the TUC guidelines
[on pay] are not observed, we shall end up with wage controls
once more and even a breakdown of democracy.'

Looking (considerably) further to the left, actress and Workers'
Revolutionary Party spokesman Vanessa Redgrave warned that
'The government were preparing concentration camps in Britain
and the army was being prepared to repress the workers in Great
Britain as it had done in Northern Ireland.'

Ask the right people, and you would find that the guilty parties
for this state of affairs lurked at every street corner: communists
and their fellow travellers, the union militants, libertarians and
pornographers, foreigners, Northern Irish Republicans, dope
fiends and drunkards, welfare scroungers, rebellious teenagers
with no moral compass, weak and spendthrift politicians and
appeasers, homosexuals, football hooligans and anyone who did
not subscribe to the *Daily Mail*, to name but a few.

The right-wing faithful would point to the history of the
Weimar Republic, whose inflation they thought Britain was
on the way towards rivalling, and which had heralded in the
evil dictatorship of Hitler. For conspiracy theorists on the left,
a more likely model was that of Chile, where a weak socialist
government gave rise to an authoritarian right-wing military
regime, and there were fears that right-wing interests might try
to politicise the British Army.

Even if the army's personnel were not being politicised (which
some thought they already were) its role certainly was being, as it
was called in to provide cover in industrial disputes involving
striking dustmen, ambulance drivers and firemen. More to the
point, the army made a show of force to guard Heathrow in 1974.

Ostensibly this was an exercise in preventing possible IRA sabotage, but senior figures within the Labour Party claim they were not forewarned of it, and suggested that it was really a dress rehearsal for a coup. Comparisons were also made with 1950s France, which had its equivalent of Northern Ireland in war-torn Algeria, along with inflation, strikes and divisions within society, all of which ushered in a 'strong man' in the form of General de Gaulle.

Just to complete the picture of paranoia, MI5 did actually bug 10 Downing Street. It originally did so at the request of then prime minister, Harold Macmillan, in 1963, in the wake of the Profumo scandal. The bugs were in place throughout the Wilson era and were only removed in 1977, on the instructions of Jim Callaghan. What is less clear is how much (or indeed whether) they were actually used.

Our Would-Be Saviours

One British military man, Brigadier Frank Kitson, wrote a book advocating training specialist bodies of troops to run essential installations like ports, railway stations and power stations in an emergency, if necessary with the use of force to keep them open. Even the mainstream press were ready to speak in what sound to us today like apocalyptic terms. This from *The Times* in 1974: 'You do not only have cranks, or shabby men in Hitler moustaches advocating an authoritarian solution. The most calm and respectable people come to believe that the only remaining choice is to impose a policy of sound money at the point of a bayonet.'

The Times also endorsed the overthrow of the aforementioned democratically elected government in Chile: 'The circumstances were such that a reasonable military man could in good faith have thought [it] his constitutional duty to intervene.'

Undemocratic thoughts were also being harboured by future Thatcherite government minister Ian Gilmore, in his 1977 book

Inside Right: 'Conservatives do not worship democracy. For them, majority rule is a device … and if it is leading to an end that is undesirable or is inconsistent with itself, then there is a theoretical case for ending it.

If some were despairing of democracy, there appeared to be no shortage of people ready to resist the forces of anarchy, if – when – the moment came. They should have been more than able to hold back the tide, if you believed their deluded estimates of the level of active popular support they commanded. One such was retired British Army General Walter Walker (1912–2001), who briefly gained fame (or was it notoriety?) in the 1970s as one of Britain's would-be saviours from the deluge. He had had an exemplary military career. Much of it was spent repressing restless foreigners in different parts of the world, ending up as Commander-in-Chief Allied Forces Northern Europe for NATO. In his retirement, he saw the need for a similarly robust approach to domestic affairs. Take, for example, his view on the unrest in Northern Ireland:

I have engaged in campaigns against blacks, yellows and slant eyes. Why should we have one rule for whites and one for coloureds? We have to decide if Northern Ireland is part of Britain or not – and if so, to act accordingly. We should cut off their petrol, gas, electricity and stop food going in, soften them up and then go in. Give warning so they can get their women and children away before we go in, but go in.

When the authorities heard that his (equally robust) views about our European allies were being sought by a television company, they had the programme banned on security grounds (or, as Walker himself put it, because he was 'revealing the true state of affairs which the politicians are hiding from the public'). But this ban did nothing to reduce his attraction as a speaker at various right-wing meetings up and down the country.

In a letter to the *Daily Telegraph* in June 1974, Walker called for 'dynamic, upgrading, invigorating leadership ... above party politics' that would 'save' the country from the 'Communist Trojan horse in our midst with its fellow travellers wriggling their maggoty way inside its belly'. To this end, Walker helped the same year to found the anti-communist Unison group (and later its offshoot Civil Assistance). He insisted that these were not, as some tried to portray them, private armies but civilian organisations, designed to underpin, not replace, the regular army in the event of a general strike. They were strike-breakers, rather than armed personnel ready to mount the barricades. Where the truth lay, between the different pictures of this and other similar groups, would – perhaps fortunately – never be put to the test.

Walker and his colleagues made ever more grandiose claims for the size of their support. By August 1974 he was claiming a membership of 100,000, with forty local controllers who were compiling a list of 'trustworthy citizens' with 'unswerving loyalty to the Crown' and 'high respect for law and order'. On the BBC's *The World at One* on 27 August he claimed membership would reach 3 million within a month and, in October, that, with each member charged with recruiting thirty others, numbers would soon pass 13.5 million.

Rather than having a military junta to which the armed forces would be responsible in an emergency, Walker saw a wider role for something like the National Association of Ratepayers' Action Groups, given suitably dynamic leadership. He also turned down the offer of help from the National Front, saying, 'I hate anything extremist.' In the event of a breakdown of law and order, where the government could not keep control of the unions, Walker had even prepared a speech he wanted the queen to read over the BBC, calling on the public to stand behind the armed forces, led in his scenario by Lord Mountbatten.

Naturally, Walker thought Harold Wilson was a proven communist and favoured Enoch Powell for prime minister. His view of Wilson may have been underpinned by 'Clockwork Orange', a campaign of misinformation run from the Information Policy Unit, working out of the Northern Ireland Army Press Office in conjunction with elements in MI5. This put out false information linking senior Labour politicians to Soviet intelligence and the IRA. One press officer who tried to expose this plot found himself framed and imprisoned for manslaughter. In these strange days, quite senior people in the Ministry of Defence found themselves openly discussing the possibility of military intervention in civil processes, should the threat of civil war seem imminent. For his part, Quentin Hogg, the Lord Chancellor, issued the guidance that it was quite lawful for the army to shoot civilians, whether or not they had been under fire themselves first.

According to the more paranoid elements in the CIA and their British adherents, the Russians, having given up on the spontaneous collapse of capitalism, were trying to undermine it from within. They believed Harold Wilson was not just a communist sympathiser but an actual KGB 'plant', put in place to become prime minister after the Russians had poisoned the previous Labour leader, Hugh Gaitskell. Their evidence for the Wilson allegations seemed to hang on nothing more than the fact that he made several trips to Russia in the 1940s as president of the Board of Trade, and several more whilst out of office as an advisor to a timber importing company, and that he numbered several 'colourful' businessmen of eastern European origin among his social circle. Even David Owen, who would become Labour Foreign Secretary, was identified by the conspiracy theorists as a Soviet spy, until someone realised they had got him mixed up with Will Owen, a left-wing Labour Member of Parliament.

Unsupported as these theories were by hard facts, many of them came from authoritative sources of paranoia. Among these were Peter Wright, an assistant director of MI5, and James Angleton, who was, until 1974, the head of the CIA's counter-intelligence division, and a man who could not look under a bed – any bed – without seeing reds. It is thought that Wright and Angleton may have got these ideas from a Soviet defector called Anatoliy Golitsyn, though the official historian of the MI5 describes him as 'an unreliable conspiracy theorist'. For their part, MI5 had maintained a file on Harold Wilson ever since his election to Parliament in 1945, but had found no evidence of a KGB link or of Soviet penetration of the Labour Party (notwithstanding John Stonehouse's links to the Czech government – see the chapter on naughty boys).

Other military men were thinking along similar lines to General Walker. This from a Major Alexander Greenwood: 'I came back from a cruise down the Rhine and discovered that England was no longer a green and pleasant land. We thought, therefore, that we would form some sort of organisation that would come in if the government failed.'

Greenwood was the founder of Red Alert, a group made up mainly of retired senior army officers and their business associates, who were 'desperately concerned about the way things were going' and keen to help out in the event of a breakdown of law and order. Yet another organiser of concerned citizenry was the war hero and founder of the Special Air Service, Colonel David Stirling. His embryonic organisation was called GB75 and, given Stirling's war record and his post-war association with mercenary groups, it is perhaps less surprising that it was again characterised as a private army. But like the others, Stirling was at pains to point out that his was simply a group of apprehensive patriots who wanted to keep the lights on in the event of something like a general strike. This may have rung a little hollow, given that most of his early recruits were former SAS colleagues and that much of the funding for it came from a millionaire arms dealer friend. Stirling himself admitted that it might be necessary for his apprehensive patriots to 'round up' any dissidents who got in the way of the smooth running of essential services. He was at the same time keen to separate GB75 from Walker's Civil Assistance, which he described as 'very right wing' and 'neo-fascist'. He also set up (with financial assistance from Sir James Goldsmith) a group dedicated to undermining trade unions, by causing as much trouble as possible during conferences. GB75 itself would have a short shelf-life, after the conventional forces of law and order ruled out any possibility of cooperation with them.

Then there was the Institute for the Study of Conflict (ISC), founded in 1970 by an ex-CIA, ex-British Intelligence man named Brian Crozier. This was a CIA-backed, right-wing propaganda group, dedicated (as their promotional material put it) 'to the defence of free industrial societies against totalitarian encroachment'. Or, as someone else described them, offering 'respectability to right-wing and repressive policies' through its 'pseudo-academic studies'. They encouraged pre-emptive police and military measures such as surveillance of suspects to combat subversion and industrial unrest, and offered training to the police and military in dealing with said subversives. Crozier was by no means an outsider. He had been a foreign correspondent for Reuters, a columnist for *The Economist* and a BBC reporter. He also had close links with the right-wing Pinochet regime in Chile and had helped them frame their new constitution. In 1988 he entered the *Guinness Book of Records* as the journalist who had interviewed more heads of state than anyone else – fifty-eight in all.

A Peaceful Revolution?

So what was the solution (if it were not to be a military takeover)? In the view of *The Times*, 'We need nothing less than a revolution in the spirit of the nation if we are to preserve the historic values of the nation ... When the crisis comes it will only be surmounted by those whom the whole nation will accept.'

But who would the whole nation accept? There would be no room in their coalition for divisive 'communist' figures like Harold Wilson or Tony Benn or for the abrasive new Conservative leader

Margaret Thatcher. *The Times'* government of national unity would be made up of people like one-nation Tories such as Edward Heath, the Liberal leader Jeremy Thorpe and Social Democrats on the right wing of the Labour Party, such as Shirley Williams, Denis Healey and Jim Callaghan. Or, as Francis Wheen put it, the very people who had got us into this mess in the first place.

Some on the right looked on with approval as Margaret Thatcher and Keith Joseph dismissed all previous Conservative governments as pale shadows of socialism, and set out to revolutionise the party. But for others, even Thatcherism was not enough, and nothing short of autocratic military rule would do.

The managing director of the Cunard shipping line, John Mitchell, was approached by military and civil service types for the loan of the *QE2* as a prison for the present Cabinet. Tony Benn learned from a senior military man of a movement – probably existing only in some fevered imaginations – called PFP ([Prince] Philip for President), in which some of the military, including members of the paratroop regiment in Northern Ireland, were said to be involved. Cecil King, the one-time chairman of International Publishing Corporation (publishers of the *Daily Mirror*) approached the head of the officer training school at Sandhurst (in front of witnesses) with the treasonable idea of them overthrowing the Labour government in favour of one of national unity, led by Lord Mountbatten.

Lord Mountbatten's role in all of this is less than clear. Was he, at one extreme, an innocent party who gave the conspirators no encouragement, or, at the other, a willing or even leading conspirator (one who was said to be privately very critical of recent government spending cuts for the armed forces)? According to Hugh Cudlipp, who was present at a meeting between King and Mountbatten at which the idea of a coup was floated, Mountbatten also described it as 'treasonable'.

While some sought to protect individual freedoms by keeping strikebound services running (or possibly by manning the barricades), others looked to the power of the courts. The National Association For Freedom (NAFF) was established in December 1975, just a week after one of its founders, Ross McWhirter, was murdered by the IRA. This was one organisation that had 'a practical mindset and genuinely potent political connections'. It also had access to some significant funding. During its involvement in the Grunwick strike it was able to raise £90,000 in just three weeks to support its strike-breaking activities. It started out as an anti-union publishing house, the Current Affairs Press, but soon diversified into getting court injunctions to stop what it saw as the excesses of trade union activity. In addition it was, over the years, opposed to: sporting boycotts related to apartheid (which it saw as a restraint of sportsmen's trade); identity cards; the European Union, and what it regarded as the left-wing bias in the BBC – it sought to have the licence fee abolished and to stop the corporation broadcasting Nelson Mandela's seventieth birthday celebrations. In 1978 (by which time they had some 20,000 members) it changed its name to the Freedom Association, to avoid possible confusion with the National Front. NAFF was the least shadowy part of the anti-union front and probably the most effective. Margaret Thatcher said that, without the support of the NAFF, Grunwick would have gone under in the face of the picketing. It was a leading member of NAFF, Robert Moss, who wrote the speech that earned Margaret Thatcher the Russian soubriquet the 'Iron Lady'.

Conspiracy in Fiction

Someone who definitely did not advocate authoritarian rule, but who was at least prepared to countenance the possibility, was playwright Howard Brenton. His drama *The Churchill Play* was set in a 1980s Britain under the dictatorship of a Labour/Conservative coalition, where journalists, trade unionists and other 'dissidents' were locked up in internment camps, modelled on that at Long Kesh in Ulster. His was only one of a number of fictional works anticipating (as one critic put it), 'Industrial confrontation, class warfare, terrorism, regional tensions, conflicts between the races and genders'.

Right-wing authoritarianism also found its way onto our television screens (at least in some people's eyes), in the form of *The Professionals*, a series of dramas about a secretive and violent special investigation unit, answerable only to the Home Secretary and not afraid to cut ethical corners in its pursuit of the baddies, in cases which fell between the remits of the police, the military and the security services.

Harold Wilson's resignation in March 1976 gave a final twist to the conspiracy theories, which now had it that he was quitting to avoid being enveloped in a scandal. But Wilson had long since given signals to his colleagues that he did not wish to serve beyond the age of 60, and he told the Cabinet of his decision five days after his sixtieth birthday. Moreover, the signs of his physical and mental deterioration from early-onset Alzheimer's had been evident to those close to him for some time.

Certainly in the final part of his premiership Wilson was convinced that right-wing (or possibly left-wing, or even both) interests were plotting against him, and there were precedents for dirty tricks dating right back to the first Labour govern-ment in 1924. Four days before the general election of that year, the *Daily Mail* published a letter purporting to come from a senior Soviet official, Grigory Zinoviev, to the Communist Party of Great Britain, calling for increased communist agitation in Britain. It is now thought to have been a forgery, but at the time was taken as genuine, and may have helped the Conservatives secure their sizeable parliamentary majority.

There was little to feed conspiracy theories in the track record of Wilson's successor, Jim Callaghan. As for his successor, Margaret Thatcher, it would be a wild-eyed conspiracy theorist indeed who accused her of communist sympathies!

12

Rupert Bare: The Oz Trial

For some people, the 1960s began on 2 November 1960, when a verdict was reached in the trial of the publishers Penguin. They were accused of obscenity in issuing copies of a hitherto forbidden novel, D.H. Lawrence's *Lady Chatterley's Lover*. Their acquittal opened the way for much greater freedom to publish adult material (or, as American senator Bronson Cutting put it, after freely acknowledging that he had not read the book, the works of 'a man with a diseased mind and a soul so black that he would obscure even the darkness of hell'). The court's decision also presaged greater freedoms in the theatre and elsewhere.

On 22 June 1971 another trial opened, which looked, as it proceeded, as if it aimed to try and claw back the freedoms won a decade before. The editors of *Oz* magazine, Richard Neville, Jim Anderson and Felix Dennis, stood accused of 'conspiring to produce a magazine containing diverse lewd, indecent and sexually perverted articles, cartoons, drawings and illustrations with intent thereby to debauch and corrupt the morals of children and young persons within the Realm and to arouse and implant in their minds lustful and perverted desires'. It was a virtual rerun of a trial to which they had been subjected (and eventually acquitted) when publishing the magazine in Australia. It would be the longest obscenity trial in British legal history.

The charge of conspiracy was one favoured by the authorities because it carried no limits to the fines or terms of imprisonment the judge could impose. Had the charge just been one of obscenity, the judge would have been limited to a £100 fine or a six-month gaol sentence. Moreover, the conspiracy charge was underpinned by a misunderstanding (whether deliberate or not) of what the 'schoolkids' edition was about. It assumed that it was a magazine written with a view to corrupting schoolkids, rather than one written *by* schoolkids. The three accused may not have fully appreciated the seriousness of their situation, since they did not make the finest first impression on the court, appearing as they did at their committal hearing in fancy dress as schoolgirls.

Oz was undoubtedly subversive and rude. As one of its contributors explained, 'Rather than inform and organise, the early underground papers were out to shriek defiance at the world of parents, school and work and bask in an alternative world of fun and dreams.' By 1970 it was reaching a circulation of 40,000 per issue. Its appeal was naturally to disaffected younger readers but, at the start of 1970, the editors were being accused of getting out of touch with their youthful audience. So it was that in February 1970, they had published the following announcement: 'Some of us at *Oz* are feeling old and boring, so we invite any readers who are under eighteen to come and edit the newspaper. You will enjoy almost complete editorial freedom. *Oz* belongs to you.'

Around twenty teenagers answered the call. Over the next few weeks they put together the April issue, focusing on the concerns and matters of interest to their age group: rock music, complaints about teachers and exams, and articles on the use of drugs (in which they saw caffeine and prescription medicines as a far greater danger than the recreational soft drugs they favoured). Much of the humour was similar to that found in college rag magazines.

But the most controversial part of the issue related to sex. Part of this dealt factually with the differing attitudes of teens to sexual activity, but perhaps the most controversial part of all was a cartoon strip which showed the comic character Rupert Bear having sexual relations with a naked granny. It was illustrated with an X-rated drawing by the underground artist Robert Crumb, onto which had been superimposed a picture of Rupert Bear's head by guest editor Vivian Berger (15). Counsel for the defence John Mortimer (he of *Rumpole* fame) asked Berger why he had done it. Berger replied: 'I think that, looking back on it, I subconsciously wanted to shock your generation; to portray us as a group of people who were different to you in moralistic attitudes. Also, it seemed to me just very funny, and like anything else that also makes fun of sex.' He added that Rupert Bear was just doing what every normal human being does, and that his montage was no different to drawings that circulated in every school classroom, every day. Berger's mother also gave evidence, saying the cartoon was a joke:

> And the joke was this; to put into print what every child knows, that is that the innocent little bear has sexual organs. Children today are surrounded by, and cannot escape from, the sexual nature of our society – newspapers which are sold by having advertisements based on sex, and which include gossip also based on innuendos about the sexual relationships between people who are not married. This is the world in which our children grow up.

The artist Feliks Topolski gave a spirited defence of the montage as 'art'. He quoted Arthur Koestler's view that unexpected elements, when brought together, produce the act of creation, of creativity – which was what this montage did. Prosecuting counsel seemed to have difficulty in thinking of the two elements together, and insisted on knowing whether Topolski thought the *Rupert Annual*, taken on its own, was art. Topolski did not, but he reiterated that the *Oz* cartoons, by bringing the two elements together, made satirical art.

In total, three whole weeks were given over to contemplating Rupert's love life in the finest detail. In one particularly fine exchange, academic Edward De Bono was asked by prosecuting counsel Brian Leary what the effect was of making Rupert so well endowed in the gentleman's department. De Bono replied that he did not know what the appropriate size should be, and the judge, Justice Michael Argyle, threatened to clear the public gallery if there was further laughter.

Leary had a bizarre exchange with social psychologist Michael Schofield, who also pointed out that the Rupert item was supposed to be a joke. 'It may not be a very good joke, but I maintain that even the funniest joke in the world would, after you, Mr Leary, had finished with it, not be very funny … The main point about it is that Rupert Bear is behaving in a way one would not expect a little bear to behave.'

This prompted Leary to ask what sort of age the witness thought the little bear was. (The correct answer at the time of the trial would have been something over 50, Rupert having first appeared, fully grown (except, perhaps, in the gentleman's department?) on the pages of the *Daily Express* in 1920. This is well above the age of consent for bears, unless they operate to very different rules to human beings.) But Leary pressed Schofield to admit that Rupert was a young bear, a schoolboy bear. Schofield replied wearily, 'I'm sorry, but I'm not as well informed as you are about little bears. I'm a psychologist. I'm supposed to look for underlying motives. But it does seem to me that you're much more expert in reading sex into things that don't immediately occur to me.'

The case had other amusing aspects, including one of those 'And who are the Beatles?' moments to which senior jurists are prone. Mishearing part of jazz singer George Melly's evidence, the judge asked him what this 'cunnilinctus' was, no doubt expecting to hear about some unexpected properties of cough medicine. Melly's answer, which included the term 'yodelling in the canyon', may have left him none the wiser. Also giving evidence for the defence was comedian Marty Feldman, who endeared himself to the judge by calling him 'a boring old fart'.

During his closing speech, Leary seemed to want to indict the whole of the permissive society, not just the three defendants. An element of paranoia was lent to the proceedings as a result of the judge receiving death threats during the course of the case. As a result, he was hidden away in a hotel under heavy armed guard for the duration. It eventually emerged that these threats came from his own unhinged committee clerk, who was sent off for psychiatric treatment. The jury took four hours to find the defendants not guilty of conspiracy, but guilty on the obscenity charges. They were remanded for medical reports, in the course of which they were forcibly shorn of their hippy locks (which caused further outrage among their supporters). The following week they were given sentences of between nine and fifteen months, to be followed by deportation, but were (unusually) given bail, pending their appeal.

They won their appeal, on the grounds that the trial judge in his summing up had thoroughly misdirected the jury (on no fewer than seventy-eight occasions, it was shown) as to the defendants' case and the definition of pornography. Another factor swaying the Lord Chief Justice was that, during the appeal hearing, he sent his clerk out into Soho to buy £20 worth of hard-core pornography. He compared this material – freely on sale – with the minor misdemeanours of the defendants, and could not understand why the case had been brought.

One reason for this dual standard would emerge later, when it transpired that the Soho vice barons had senior and junior officers of the Flying Squad and the Obscene Publications Squad on their payroll. Over 400 officers were prosecuted, sacked or pushed into early retirement in the purge that followed. The case gave *Oz* the sort of publicity that publishers can only dream of. For a time, the circulation doubled, to 80,000. However, it faded again and the loss-making publication breathed its last in November 1973.

In 1995, Judge Argyle compounded his errors by writing a magazine article in which he libelled Felix Dennis. Dennis sued the magazine and secured a substantial donation to charity from it. He was only deterred from suing the judge himself by Argyle's advanced age (he was by then in his eighties).

13

And Another
Thing ...

This final chapter gives us a chance to cover those stories that did
not fit neatly anywhere else in the book.

Let Me Out!

Nowadays there are concerns in some quarters about Britain
being overwhelmed by the numbers of immigrants coming into
this country. Back in the 1970s, the concern was rather from
other countries, fearful of being swamped by a tidal wave of
Brits fleeing the country's economic and other woes. By 1974
New Zealand, a country of just 3 million people, was receiving
25,000 British immigrants a year. It was putting such a strain on
the housing supply, jobs and public services that the government
had to introduce a cap on immigration. Australia did the same
thing the following year, as applications from Britain rose by
50 per cent. As opportunities in these countries declined, more
people looked to Canada (applications up 65 per cent) and South
Africa (29,000 people from the 'managerial classes' went there in
a single year). Overall in 1975, 269,000 people emigrated, while
only 184,000 came into Britain. Britain's population fell, for the
first time since records began, and continued to do so over the
following two years. But even those who emigrated were the tip
of a much larger iceberg. A survey in 1977 suggested that one

in three of those interviewed would like to leave the country
(including half of all those under 25). As an aside, during the
first two weeks of the three-day week in 1974 the New Zealand
High Commission reported a trebling in the number of people
enquiring about emigration from Britain.

Let Me In! Foreign Food Takes Over

Mass immigration from the Commonwealth had become a
controversial issue by the 1970s (despite the fact that, as we
have seen, for a good part of the decade there were more people
leaving the country than coming in). By 1981 the census recorded
2.2 million Commonwealth immigrants in Britain. Apart from
anything else, it meant that a sea-change in our eating habits was
under way. By the mid-1970s most towns had their Indian or
Chinese restaurants. In fact one restaurant in eight was serving
'foreign' food (however that is defined) and, by 1977, there were
more Chinese takeaways than fish and chip shops in our high
streets. What's more, the British were washing it down with more
foreign stuff – wine! In 1973, the average Briton drank nine pints
of wine a year; by 1980, this had risen to almost twenty.

Law and Disorder

In 1972, a new word graced the nation's media – mugging.
(Actually, it had been around for a lot longer – it appears to
derive from a sixteenth-century Scandinavian term for 'striking
someone in the face'.) It meant an assault on a person with
intention to rob, and was brought to prominence by the death of
an elderly widower, Arthur Hills. The offence (if not the actual
term) had been created by the Theft Act 1968, as a form of
robbery. It could carry a sentence of up to life imprisonment but,
to qualify as robbery rather than theft, the threat of violence had
to be immediate, rather than at some time in the future. In 1972,

violent crime had risen by 62 per cent in five years, and it had almost doubled by the end of the decade. Sensational press coverage, combined with an element of racist sentiment, ensured that the offence quickly became high profile.

One early victim of mugging was the television presenter Robin Day, who was unable to talk his way out of a broken jaw and a black eye. Reginald Maudling, the Home Secretary, joined the nation in lamenting the trend, seeing 'the crumbling of discipline, the growth of crime and the apparent erosion of the sense of personal responsibility', something that he attributed to the disappearance of the 'old disciplines of mass unemployment and grinding poverty'. A bit more mass unemployment and grinding poverty – that's what the nation needed!

Something else you were likely to be arrested for was being the wrong colour, for the police were having real difficulty adjusting to the idea of a multi-racial society. To start with, the force was not representative of the communities it served. In 1972, there were only fifty-eight black and Asian policemen in the whole of England and Wales, out of a total force of over 110,000. The head of the Metropolitan Police, Sir Robert Mark, launched a recruitment drive aimed at these groups, with the slogan, 'the only colour we recognise is blue'. It did not do much good: by the end of the decade there were still only 286 black and Asian policemen nationwide, and a number of those complained about their treatment at the hands of racist colleagues.

However, what really alienated the police from the black community was the so-called 'sus law' (short for 'suspected person'). This was based on the Vagrancy Act of 1824, which said that any 'suspected person or reputed thief' frequenting – well, virtually anywhere – 'shall be deemed a rogue and a vagabond' and could be found guilty of an offence carrying up to three months' imprisonment. In short, the police could stop, search and potentially arrest anyone they thought guilty of 'frequenting'. But the ones they chose to stop were disproportionately black. In 1976, some four out of every ten people arrested under this power were black, despite black people only making up 2 per cent of the nation's population at that time. The Metropolitan Police were by far the greatest users of the law, bringing over half the nation's prosecutions and, in 1975, black Londoners were more than fifteen times more likely to be arrested for petty theft. Another, smaller group who were disproportionately stopped were apparently punks.

The use of this law gave rise to widespread protest and the relevant section of the Vagrancy Act was repealed in 1981. For a long time the police did not have to keep records of stopping and searching people (arrests were obviously recorded) but this was tightened up by the 1984 Police and Criminal Evidence Act. This required the police to keep records of people being stopped and searched (but not those simply stopped) and also tightened up the criteria for using stop and search – skin colour and manner of dress were no longer supposed to be sufficient grounds for suspicion. Even so, in 2005–6 black Londoners were still more than seven times more likely to be stopped and searched than their white counterparts.

Phew, What a Scorcher!

The summer of 1976 was the hottest since records began. Every day between 22 June and 16 July daytime temperatures exceeded 80°F and on fifteen consecutive days it was over 90° somewhere in Britain. On five days it exceeded 95°. At Wimbledon, temperatures on court soared to 104° and even the reserved British spectators started taking their shirts off. Ice cream prices reached unprecedented levels and food prices generally soared, as crops worth £500 million wilted and died in the fields. With some areas going forty-five days without a drop of rain there was a chronic water shortage. Some reservoirs ran completely dry, as did many rivers and streams around the country. Tinder-dry forests and heaths went up in almost uncontrollable fires, with firemen in some areas

working seventy-two-hour shifts to tackle them. Some areas were reduced to getting their water from standpipes and in South Wales water supplies were cut off completely for part of the day. That summer, the AA was called out by some 1,500 motorists with over-heating engines, and you could be fined £400 simply for washing your car. A Drought Act was rushed through Parliament and Denis Howell was appointed minister for droughts. He told us all to put a brick in our cisterns and share a bath with our wives (government policy for single people was kept tantalisingly vague). Inevitably, the minister was scarcely in post before the weather changed dramatically. September and October were both exceptionally wet months and normal meteorological service was resumed.

Jet City

At the time of writing this the nation is locked in a seemingly inter-minable debate about the future of air travel to and from London, and one of the options being proposed – and championed by the Mayor of London – is a gigantic new airport built on an island in the Thames estuary. Just such an airport was very nearly built in the 1970s and, had things been just a little different, people could today be talking about flying from Maplin, rather than Heathrow.

As long ago as 1960, noise at Heathrow was enough of a problem to warrant a government committee, which proposed that other airports be provided near London to take some of the demand away from it. An exhaustive and exhausting planning process came up in 1971 with the preferred site of Cublington in Buckinghamshire. But this fell foul of influential local political pressure and the eminent planner Colin Buchanan came up with what looked to be an environmentally more acceptable alternative.

Maplin Sands (also known as Foulness) was a sandbank in the Thames estuary, used by the military for artillery practice. In April 1971, the government announced that it was ignoring the careful deliberations of its own commission and going ahead instead with Maplin. For a while, it looked like that rarest of planning phenomena – an airport proposal that everybody could agree upon – and the process appeared to be going ahead at full speed. The military started retrieving their unexploded shells from the sands, a development authority was set up with powers to borrow £250 million and they even started moving the sands about, the first stage in creating an airport-shaped island in the Thames. There was a precedent for the scheme – the Dutch had created Schipol airport on just such an island in the North Sea.

The scheme was nothing if not ambitious. As well as a four-runway airport there was to be a supertanker and container-ship terminal (since these vessels were getting too big to dock further up the Thames) and a new town (or 'jet city' as some overwrought MPs were wont to call it) with a final population of over 300,000. All of these would be linked to London by an eight-lane motorway and a high-speed railway. Over 70,000 jobs would be directly created by the scheme, and many more in the economic boom for Essex that would flow from it. The promise of all these jobs bought off local authority opposition, and local protest was originally relatively small-scale and muted.

The building of all this would naturally take some time. Original timetables had the first runway opening in 1975 or 1976, but with building works running on to 'the turn of the century or beyond'. Meanwhile, opposition to it began to build. In the Commons, Labour came out against it (rather than Jet City, they called the new town 'Heathograd'). There was also Conservative parliamentary opposition from some quarters. These included a relatively young Essex MP (and former airline pilot) named Norman Tebbit. Also, the noise implications were said to be worse than originally thought; the island's population of Brent geese would be badly affected (especially those that got sucked into jet aircraft engines) and the loss of the island's shellfish beds would bring the nation's balance of payments to its knees by necessitating cockles to be imported.

More pertinently, the case was made that the airport would damage London's East End – the programme got delayed and (in line with every other major civil-engineering project in history) the estimated costs began to escalate. Add to this Britain's worsening economic prospects and the impact of the oil crisis on civil air traffic forecasts, and even the scheme's supporters began to have doubts. In January 1974, the government announced a 'wide-ranging and comprehensive' review of the scheme, but it was left to its Labour successors in power formally to cancel it.

The Poster that Worked

One of the most famous political posters of the 1970s was prepared for the Conservatives in the run-up to the 1979 general election. It was designed by their new advertising agency Saatchi and Saatchi and broke many of the conventional rules of such advertising. It did not mention the Conservatives or their new leader Margaret Thatcher at all, though their opponents' name featured large on it. It said nothing about Conservative values or what they would do to tackle the problem they were highlighting. And the issue on which they chose to take on that opposition – unemployment – was traditionally regarded as one of Labour's stronger suits. It just showed a long queue of people snaking into the unemployment office along with the words 'Labour isn't working'. Not even Saatchis were sure about this, and almost dropped it from the options they presented to their clients. Margaret Thatcher's first reaction to it was 'We're advertising Labour.' Initially, shortage of money meant they could only post it on twenty sites across the country, but Labour got suckered into a row about it in the media, which guaranteed the Conservatives more coverage than they could have dreamed of.

And where did all these poor huddled masses in the queue come from? They were volunteers from the Hendon branch of the Young Conservatives and their families – and apparently not one of them was unemployed. There were not enough of them to make a suitably impressive queue so – thanks to the magic of photography – some of them appear up to five times in the line-up. For their part, Labour had a billboard harking back to the three-day week, showing a candle and the slogan, 'Remember the last time the Tories said they had all the answers?' – but who remembers that poster?

Milton Keynes

There was one place in north Buckinghamshire that epitomised the way in which Britain was changing in the 1970s. New towns had been a flagship policy of the post-war Attlee Labour government and had incorporated elements of collectivist policy in their design – such as a reliance on public transport (Bracknell new town was one of those that grossly under-provided for the growth in car ownership) and an emphasis on rented, rather than owner-occupied, housing. Milton Keynes started off the same way. Originally designed as a linear city, it was to be built around a series of futuristic ratepayer-funded monorail routes, with many of its planned 250,000 residents living in rented housing and government limits on who could live there. Private open space would be limited; there would be much more emphasis on the public realm.

But by 1971, as the first houses were being completed, it was becoming clear that this was no longer how people wanted to live and the design team radically changed the nature of the town. It became instead a more dispersed American-style grid-iron of streets, with car traffic managed within each grid square. It became more consumerist than collectivist, with the shopping centre planned to be built in advance of facilities like a hospital or a railway station. (In fact, the shopping centre did not open until 1979.) The new town's development struggled in the early years, due to labour and materials shortages and industrial disputes, not to mention the Dutch elm disease and 1976 drought, which together wiped out a lot of the landscaping. But it was successful in attracting employment, and that in turn generated interest in living there. For once, this new town was going to be open to all, rather than being exclusively overspill for a particular town or city.

The move from rented to owner-occupied housing came about rather less quickly. By 1979 there were still only 13,000 owner-occupied homes in the town; it was under the Conservative governments of the 1980s that the sale of houses really gathered pace. Margaret Thatcher came to open the shopping centre shortly after becoming prime minister, and her next port of call was the home of a couple who were buying their home from the development corporation.

Let There be Light ...

There are lots of festivals of lights; the Hindus, Sikhs and Jains have Diwali, the Jews Hanukkah and the Buddhists Tazaungdaing. (The turning on of Blackpool illuminations for the Kissmequickists doesn't count.) The one we are interested in is the Nationwide Festival of Light, a British Christian initiative launched in the early 1970s. It started when a couple of young Christian missionaries, Peter and Janet Hill, returned to England after four years of evangelical work in India. They were shocked at the more permissive society they found on their return, in terms of sex, violence, tolerance of abortion and homosexuality and 'other manifestations of the nation's falling away from God'. They began to lobby for proper Christian moral standards to be restored.

They naturally got a warm reception from what some might call the religious right – such as Mary Whitehouse, Malcolm Muggeridge, Lord Longford and Cliff Richard – and from a number of Christian denominations and sympathetic celebrities. A committee was formed, which coined the name the 'Nationwide Festival of Light', and even Prince Charles sent them 'every good wish for the success of the festival'.

The movement had two aims: one was to protest against the exploitation of sex in the media and the arts; the other, to offer Christian teaching as a restorative for moral sanity. Herein lay one of the movement's problems, for there were significant numbers of people who shared the concern about 'sexploitation', but who did not sign up to the Christian baggage associated with the campaign. They would rather see the campaign cast in religiously neutral terms. Another dilemma for the movement was whether they should seek stricter censorship through legislation, or by voluntary agreements applied by persuasion.

Their first major public meeting was in Westminster Central Hall on 9 September 1971. It was infiltrated by the Gay Liberation Front (dressed as nuns) who did their best to disrupt the meeting by releasing mice, blowing horns and turning the lights off, but the speakers still managed to make some passionate denunciations of sex and violence. This was followed by some seventy regional rallies around the country. In Bristol they had the target of a sex supermarket opening in the city; in Sheffield there was Cliff Richard lighting a calor-gas flare, one of around 300 lit up and down the country.

On 25 September a national rally was held in Trafalgar Square. A crowd, variously estimated at anywhere between 30,000 and 40,000 (two-thirds of the crowd were thought to be under 25) listened to more than a dozen speakers denigrate the exploitation of sex and violence. They warned that love and respect for the individual and the family were under threat, with the collapse of a safe and stable society not far behind. The crowd then proceeded to Hyde Park, where a Christian concert was laid on for them. The main speaker there was American street evangelist Arthur Blessitt, whose claim to fame involved travelling the world carrying a 12ft wooden cross.

How do you follow an event on that scale? After that, the movement seemed rather to lose its way. It gradually evolved (by 1983) into CARE (Christian Action Research and Education) and gave up its confrontational approach in favour of social work among those whose lives have been affected by the social and moral breakdown. It is difficult to detect any significant long-term impact of the movement on the media or wider society.

She Who Must be Dismayed and the BBC

Although her campaign to clean up the public realm began in the 1960s, Mary Whitehouse was rarely out of the public eye throughout the 1970s. Her main target was the nest of communists in control of the BBC, who she believed were in cahoots with bodies such as the National Council for Civil Liberties, the Communist Party and the Campaign for Homosexual Equality in a plot to undermine conventional morality. (Homosexuality, she believed, was a curable disease.) She regularly attacked the BBC and its liberal head, Hugh Carlton Greene, for 'peddling the propaganda of disbelief, doubt and dirt' and celebrating 'promiscuity, infidelity and drinking'. In her view, people watched BBC programmes 'at the risk of serious damage to their morals, their patriotism, their discipline and their family life'.

Few programmes (*Dixon of Dock Green* and the snooker aside) escaped her critical gaze. Alf Garnett was criticised, not for his racist and reactionary views, but for his use of no fewer than 121 'bloodies' in a half-hour show. (Alf's creator Johnny Speight later referred to her and her colleagues in a publication as 'fascists' and was successfully sued by her. He in turn got his revenge in an episode in which Alf read Whitehouse's book *Cleaning up Television* with great approval before his daughter and son-in-law burnt it, chanting 'Unclean, unclean'.) Comedian Dave Allen was held to be disrespectful towards the Catholic Church, and *It Ain't Half Hot Mum* and *Some Mothers Do 'Ave 'Em* were guilty of constant sexual innuendo ('It seemed that the male sex organ was the in thing,' she complained).

She successfully got Alice Cooper's record 'School's Out' banned from *Top of the Pops* for inciting violence; Cooper later sent her flowers in thanks for the publicity she generated, which helped propel the record to Number 1 in the charts. She also objected to Chuck Berry's 'My Ding-a-Ling' appearing on the same programme (despite the song's lyrics pointing out that the ding-a-ling referred to was nothing more than 'silver bells hanging on a string'). Ironically, she did, however, give *Top of the Pops* presenter Jimmy Savile a special award for 'wholesome family entertainment' in his *Jim'll Fix It* programme.

Some of her targets were less predictable. *Dr Who* came in for particular criticism, as being full of 'the sickest and most horrible material – obscene violence and horror'. She particularly took offence at one episode which featured 'strangulation – by hand, claw, by obscene vegetable matter'. For good measure, one episode even showed the tiny tots how to make a Molotov cocktail. A documentary showing the liberation of Belsen concentration camp was classed as 'filth', because it was 'an awful intrusion' that was 'bound to shock and offend' and was 'very offputting'. Even the innocuous children's puppets Pinky and Perky triggered a letter of complaint to the BBC about the puppets' 'callous attitude towards their human co-star'. For its part the BBC took the opportunity to send her up – the Goodies devoted an episode to satirising her, and an entire series – *Swizzlewick* – starred a thinly disguised parody of a Mary Whitehouse figure. She may have been easy to mock, but she spoke for a significant body of opinion. At its peak, her National Viewers' and Listeners' Association had a membership of over 31,000 (as many as the Communist Party of Great Britain and almost twice that of the National Front) and her petition for public decency attracted some 1.35 million signatures. Small wonder that Harold Wilson's staff used to 'lose' her letters to the prime minister, rather than have to reply to them.

Miss Festival Bikini?

Who would have thought that the worthy Festival of Britain would have given rise to one of the most avidly watched – and widely criticised – of entertainment institutions, one that would still be going strong over sixty years later? The Festival Bikini Contest was organised in 1951 by Eric Morley as a one-off event for the festival, and was only continued when news came in of someone else stealing the idea. The bikini part of it had to be dropped after 1951 in favour of something more modest, after this new-fangled

form of swimwear proved too revealing for some of the more conservative competitors. The name *Miss World* was given to the contest by the media from the start. It was televised from 1959 and in 1968 attracted the year's highest British audience of 27.5 million (the sort of viewing figures normally reserved for royal weddings).

The 1970s saw both the height of the contest's popularity and its most controversial period. The 1970 ceremony was infiltrated by feminists, who attacked it – and the host, Bob Hope – with flour bombs, stink bombs and water pistols. Hope later claimed that his assailants were all on drugs. A further dimension to the controversy was provided by apartheid South Africa, which for much of the 1970s entered both a white candidate (Miss South Africa) and a black one (Miss Africa South). In 1970, liberal opinion may have derived a certain – very quali-fied – pleasure from the fact that Miss Africa South was runner up, behind another black candidate, from Grenada. From 1976 several countries boycotted the contest in protest against South Africa's dual entries, and South Africa itself dropped out from 1977 until the fall of apartheid. There was a United Kingdom victory in 1974, but only until it was discovered that she was a single parent. The rules only said that you had to be single to enter but, according to the unwritten moral code operated by the organisers, single naturally implied childless.

Attempts have been made over the years to bring the contest more into line with modern thinking. The judges' inspection of the candidates' posteriors was dropped in 1975, following protests, and new rounds have been introduced to try and test their person-ality, stage presence and public-speaking skills. More particularly, from 1972 the organisers set up Beauty with a Purpose, a charity which has generated hundreds of millions for disadvantaged children. Nonetheless, the major broadcasters in Britain decided it had had its day, and stopped broadcasting it from 1988. Elsewhere its popularity seemed to be undimmed, and it attracted a world-wide audience of 2.5 billion in 155 countries in 1997.

Many of the winning contestants have in fact gone on to carve out distinguished careers for themselves, as doctors, diplomats, jazz musicians, writers, journalists and in charity work. But surely none can rival the achievement of 1975 winner Wilnelia Merced of Puerto Rico, who went on to become the third Mrs Bruce Forsyth. Mr Forsyth seems to have a bit of a thing about beauty contests, for it was at a Miss Lovely Legs contest that he met Anthea Redfern, who became his co-host on the *Generation Game* and then his second wife.

Pub Bombers

November 1974 saw a spate of pub bombings in Birmingham, that left twenty-one people killed and 182 injured. The attacks were apparently unrelated to military targets; there were no military establishments nearby, and some of the carnage was so horrific that the police refused to allow the media to film at the scenes. The attacks led to a wave of anti-Irish feeling in the country. Irish people found themselves turned off buses, refused service in shops and threatened in pubs, and some buildings with Irish connections were petrol bombed. There were fears that the backlash could escalate into serious anti-Catholicism, but it turned out that all Irish, of whatever religious persuasion, were the targets.

Home Secretary Roy Jenkins had to be seen to be doing something, to prevent mob rule taking hold. At high speed, and with the support of the Conservative opposition, the Prevention of Terrorism Act was passed into law. It gave the government powers to deport foreigners involved in terrorism, made it a criminal offence to belong to or support the IRA and gave the police powers to detain and question people from Ireland for up to seven days. Most of these measures were relatively moderate (and some, like the ban on supporting the IRA, were almost impossible to apply), but they managed to assuage public outrage enough to prevent vigilantism, without getting civil libertarians too annoyed. More radical measures, like the reintroduction of the death penalty and the public demand for identity cards (the latter of which, in particular, would have been difficult and expensive to implement) did not come to anything.

Unfortunately, the same moderation did not apply to elements within the police force, who beat 'confessions' for the bombings out of six long-standing Birmingham residents of Irish extraction. They served sixteen years of a life sentence before being released in 1991. As a result, the Birmingham pub bombings are remembered today less as a murderous and random act of terror and more for the miscarriage of justice that followed. The real guilty parties were never found.